W A.

Spring Buds and Autumn Leaves

Poems

W A.

Spring Buds and Autumn Leaves
Poems

ISBN/EAN: 9783337005658

Printed in Europe, USA, Canada, Australia, Japan

Cover: Foto ©Thomas Meinert / pixelio.de

More available books at **www.hansebooks.com**

SPRING BUDS

AND

AUTUMN LEAVES.

Poems.

BY

A. W.

LONDON:
HURST AND BLACKETT, PUBLISHERS,
SUCCESSORS TO HENRY COLBURN,
13, GREAT MARLBOROUGH STREET.
1860.

CONTENTS.

	PAGE
Prefatory Verses	1
Time was, Time is, Time shall be	3
Spring	6
To the Moon	8
Life's Young Dream	10
Sir Eldred. A Ballad	11
The Forsaken	20
Impromptu	22
To the Westwood Oak	23
The Forced Smile	26
To the Last Rose	27
To the Stars	29
Impromptu. Written on the Sand	31
January 1st, 1837	32
The Departure of the Swallows	34
The Desolate Heart	36
Autumn Flowers	38
A Sketch. Drawn from Life by the Sea-Shore—The Fisher's Wife	40
Farewell to the Old Year, 1852	45
Reminiscences	47

vi   CONTENTS.

                                                              PAGE
Sonnet.   The Nameless Grave   51
Stanzas 52
To ——   54
To illustrate a Painting of two Frogs sitting under a
        Mushroom 55
Recipe for a Scent Jar.   59
To the Bee   61
On Reading some Lines in Censure of the late Lord
        Byron   63
Sonnet.   To Night 66
To my Brother, A. J., with Flowers   67
Lines written in the long Winter of 1814   .   . 70
Alone.   72
Farewell to 1858   74
" I Loathe it, I Loathe it.   I would not Live always "   76
To my Foster-Child in Heaven   78
" She is not Dead, but Sleepeth "   .   .   .   81
Retrospection 83
Composed in a Garden   85
Stanzas for Sacred Music   88
Composed in the Prospect of an Unexpected Recovery
        from Illness   89
Summer Evening by the Sea-Shore 92
To C. C.   94
The Farewell 96
Impromptu.   To S. T., on her Birthday, 1822 .   97
Sonnet 99
To the Robin   100
She Mourneth in Secret .   .   . 102
Impromptu   103

		PAGE
A Boat Song. Set to Music	.	104
Translated from the French	. . . . .	106
Stanzas set to Music	. . . . . .	107
To F——, with a Kettle-Holder, on the 14th of February	. . . . . .	108
Stanzas adapted to Music	. . . . .	109
Composed on Hearing the Bells on Christmas Morning, 1859.	. . . . . .	110
Solemn Musings	. . . . .	112
Composed in Sickness.	. . . . .	116
A Ballad.	. . . . . .	118
To ——	. . . . . .	135

JUVENILE POEMS,

PRINCIPALLY WRITTEN BETWEEN THE AGE OF TEN AND SIXTEEN YEARS.

On the Death of my Beloved Mother. Composed in my Tenth Year	 137
Farewell to a Favourite Nurse	 139
Alwyn and Evelina. A Fact versified in my Eleventh Year	 141
The Flower Garden	 144
To a Robin which dropped on the Floor in a Half-frozen State	 147
On seeing Children Building Houses with Cards	. 149
On a Heartsease that Bloomed through the Year	. 151
To M. M., with Violets	 154
To Laura. An Invocation to rise	. . . 155
On the Deserted Cottage on Danwick Cliff.	. . 157

PAGE

To Spring 159
To Mary 161
Elegy on a Pet Leveret 162
A Satire in Imitation of Horace.   Impromptu . 164
To a Friend with the First Violet . . . 166
"The Wind passeth over it, and it is gone" . . 168
To Mary, with a Basket of Flowers. . . . 170
Impromptu 172
Lines 173
Supposed to be Written by a Disappointed Lover . 174
Love's Logic 176
Little Alice.   A Riddle 178

ORIGINAL ENIGMAS, CHARADES, ETC.

Enigmas 181
Charades 192
Rebuses 206

PREFATORY VERSES.

Go, little Barque, trembling I send thee forth,
  My first bold venture on the shoreless deep :
Although thy freightage be of little worth,
  Yet on thy course an anxious watch I keep.

Alas thy merchandize hath cost me dear.
  I culled " *Spring Buds*" while calmer spirits slept,
And " *Autumn's* falling *Leaves*" collected here,
  With many a pang of fond regret were swept.

Light is thy cargo, may fair breezes speed
  Thee on thy way, nor shoal, nor fatal rock,
Nor statelier craft, thy buoyant course impede,
  And bear thee down, with overwhelming shock.

                                                    B

Poor little Barque! thy frame is wondrous slight,

   And should the awful Board that scans thee o'er,

Pronounce thee not sea-worthy, trim, nor tight,

   Thy Builder will not launch thee from the shore,

   But break thy timbers up, and never trust thee

     more.

SPRING BUDS AND AUTUMN LEAVES.

TIME WAS, TIME IS, TIME SHALL BE.

TIME was, when my young heart, unscathed by care,
   Leapt forth with joy to greet the coming year:
Gay, smiling Hope hung her bright garlands there,
   And bade the unknown hours all light appear;
   And if perchance mine eye confessed a tear,
'Twas a fond tribute to the parting one,
   One whose sweet memory was passing dear,
As thoughts that hover o'er a friend long known,
To look with smiles upon us, now for ever gone!

Time was, when, in the stillness of the night,
   Mine ear kept vigil for the sweet bell's tone,
That waked the new-born year, and told the flight,
   The instant flight of the departing one,
   Thou sweet sad requiem of moments gone!

What said thy warning voice to my young heart ?
  Did it not whisper of fond hopes o'erthrown ?
Did it not raise, with necromantic art,
Phantoms of wasted hours, making pale conscience
      start ?

Yes, but these sage reflections on the past
  Soon yielded to the light and buoyant play
Of untired spirits, and were rudely cast.
  E'en as a noisome weed, away—away !
    Then came the dream of joys that might not stay,
Vain earthborn visions ! cheaters of the brain !
    Fret-work of fancy ! that one lucid ray
Had melted into nothingness again.
But young hearts will not brook stern reason's
      sober rein.

Time is, when Fancy's wild creations sink
  Beneath the touch of cold reality,
When tried experience trembles on the brink
  Of time gone by, and *that* which is to be,
  For in prophetic vision he can see
The future as the past, with sorrows rife,
  The serpent sin, in dread vitality,
Shudd'ring he views, with crest uppreared for strife,
Or coiled amidst the flowers that would embellish
      life.

Time shall be, when this restless, changing scene
   Of mortal conflict, this perturbed day,
To me shall be as if it ne'er had been,
   And hope and fear alike shall pass away :
   Aye, soon shall vanish all this bright array,
This gorgeous pageantry of earth and sky.
   Then, oh, my soul, amid the wide decay,
The crash of spheres, the wreck of vanity,
Look up with joy, for thy redemption draweth nigh.

SPRING.

'Tis Spring-tide, and each lovely bloom,
    That slept the wintry night away,
Now springs exulting from its tomb,
    And laughing meets the genial ray.

Each bright eye gazes on the sun,
    Each woos him with expanded breast,
And when his farewell beam is gone,
    Each folds her rich embroidered vest.

They weep all night their gentle tears,
    Their soft eyes closed, resigned and meek,
Till their loved golden beam appears,
    Kindling new beauty on their cheek.

Fair worshippers! their fragrant sighs,
    As clouds of grateful incense spread,
While their bright Parent from the skies
    Showers dewy blessings on their head.

Afar the playful breeze has borne
  The honied breath of fairest flowers;
Hark! how the *wild* bee winds his horn,
  And revels mid the scented bowers.

All nature seems with gladness rife,
  The *wild* birds trill their raptured lay,
And countless forms of insect life
  Spread their glad wings and dart away.

Oh! Spring, I love thy hopeful time!
  Thy budding sprays, thy skies of blue,
Thou emblem of my youthful prime,
  When all was bright, and fresh, and new!

Summer unfolds her peerless rose,
  But canker-worms oft mar the bloom;
And Autumn with bright fruitage glows,
  But falling leaves prepare her tomb.

Sweet Spring! all changeful as thou art,
  I care not for thy passing frown;
I clasp thy promise to my heart,
  For smiling Hope is all thy own.

TO THE MOON

Yes, thou art fair, sweet Moon, to-night,
And yet methinks thou'rt far less bright
    Than when I saw thee last;
Thy smile illumes as calm a sea,
And quiet hills, as when on thee
    I gazed in moments past.

But there were eyes whose blessed light
Made thine appear more softly bright
    Than e'er it did before;
Gone are those eyes, beloved rays,
Alone upon thine orb I gaze,
    And think thee bright no more.

Ye few sweet moments of our day,
Ye treasured few, of transient stay,
    That flit on rainbow wing:
Dancing in pleasure's meteor ray,
Fair flowers that bloom in life's dull way,
    What bitterness ye bring!

The light-winged breath of Summer throws
His balmy freshness o'er the rose,
    And then pursues his flight,
Yet oft returns the wayward power,
To revel with the happy flower;
    But ye have left me quite—

Quite left me, and her magic art,
To soothe the sorrow of my heart,
    Fond memory tries in vain;
Alas! her tale of pleasures o'er,
Can only make me weep the more,
    And wish them mine again.

LIFE'S YOUNG DREAM.

Farewell sweet dream ! 'tis bitterness to part
  With thee, sweet dream, the solace of long years,
Like a fair flower entwining round my heart,
  In its sweet bloom absorbing all my tears,
' Or as the western beam at evening peers
Through parting clouds that wept the morn away,
  So that thought's sunshine brightened through
      my fears,
And cheered my spirit with its blessed ray,
Ah! wherefore must I mourn, sweet dream, thy
      broken sway.

SIR ELDRED.

A BALLAD.

" Oh! why dost thou turn from the dark green wood?
'   And why is thy cheek so pale ?
And why must we cross that perilous flood,
   That heaves to the midnight gale ?"

" Oh, Lady ! I turn with a thrilling dread,
   When the moon is riding high ;
For shadowy forms in that dark green shade
   Are nightly gliding by.

" Yon hawthorn, which brightened the hill's dark
      brow,
   When the silvery radiance shone,
And looks like a moving mass of snow,
   Now the clouds sail over the moon—

" When beauty has passed from the wintry bowers,
   And fields no more are green,
That hawthorn all white with its pearly flowers,
   As in pride of May is seen.

"Though all the winds of heaven should sleep,
  And no breath sweep over the hill;
That hawthorn will tremble and bow o'er the steep,
  And toss its white garland still.

"They tell of a knight and a youthful maid,
  A lady of noble degree,
Who oft-times stole through the secret shade,
  And met 'neath the hawthorn tree.

"Oh! the maid was fair as that snowy bell
  That droops in the dewy vale;
The knight was brave, and he loved her well;
  Now, Lady, give ear to my tale."

Fair Leonore leaned on her lover's breast,
  And her tears were falling fast,
For Sir Eldred had donned his warrior vest,
  And he came to woo his last.

"Oh, Leonore!" sighed the enamoured knight,
  "Wilt thou love me when far away?
When thy Eldred no longer can visit thy sight,
  Will his form in thy memory stay?"

"Believe," said the maid, "though thine absence be
  Until youth and hope be flown;
My tenderest thought shall be given to thee,
  I will love but thee alone."

"Oh! wilt thou forgive, dear maid, if I yield
  To a lover's jealous fears!
Should thy warrior fall on the battle field,
  Wilt thou soon forget thy tears?"

"Oh, Eldred!" she murmured with shuddering
        breath,
  "May mercy avert that blow,
These eyes must close in the sleep of death,
  Ere for Eldred they cease to flow."

"When the lord of the valley beholds thy face,
  Thy beauty will make him sigh,
And the lord of the valley has every grace
  That can tempt a maiden's eye.

"Fair is the fame, and high the degree
  Of that young and wealthy lord.
While thy soldier's sole merit is loving thee,
  And his wealth lies in his sword."

A frown came over her lovely brow,
  As a cloud comes over the moon;
And her fair cheek flushed with a crimson glow,
  But the frown and the blush fled soon.

She frowned with a feeling of maiden pride,
  Her lover's distrust to blame;
But he gazed in her eyes till resentment died.
  And she blushed from maiden shame.

" When Leonore, faithless to love and thee,
     To another shall plight her vow,
This hawthorn, to witness her perfidy,
     Shall bloom 'mid December's snow."

"Then give me a tress of thy golden hair,
     As a pledge, before we part ;
No earthly power shall the treasure tear
     From thy Eldred's faithful heart."

She loosed the chaplet that bound her hair,
     And her locks fell in golden showers,
And they played on her cheek and her bosom fair,
     As sunbeams amid the flowers.

Then she raised a ringlet from Eldred's brow,
     With her fingers so taper and white,
And they gleamed like mountain-peaks of snow
     'Mid the sable clouds of night.

" Now twine them together in mystic braid,
     And vow thou wilt never forget,
'Till this raven lock change to a silvery grey,
     And this golden be black as jet."

" I twine them together," replied the maid,
     " And vow I will never forget
'Till thy raven lock change to a silvery grey,
     And my golden be black as jet."

As she gave him the token, a sound of fear
  Stole over the peaceful vale ;
Sir Eldred's eye kindled, that sound to hear,
  But Leonore's cheek grew pale.

'Tis the trumpet's call ! the hour is come !
  No longer the parting delay,
One farewell embrace—hark—yonder's the drum,
  Fond lover, away—away !

Like the roebuck he sprang from the hawthorn shade,
  Nor lingered to falter adieu !
But he waved his plumed helm to the sorrowing maid,
  Ere the deep wood concealed him from view.

The lord of the valley came over the hill
  While the lady was yet in her woe ;
He sprang from his steed, and stole softly and still
  Behind the o'ershadowing bough.

He gazed as she leaned on her snowy arm
  And her hair as a curtain of gold,
Half veiling her features and elegant form,
  Was floating in many a fold.

He gazed with emotion on Leonore's tears,
  He gazed and he fondly admired ;
But lest his bold presence should waken her fears,
  He unseen and in silence retired.

The lord of the valley no rest could know
   'Till he sought for that fair one's love ;
But Leonore, true to her plighted vow,
   Nor sighs nor entreaties could move.

They tell how this comely and wealthy young lord
   Fell sick for the maid of the vale ;
How he fled from his friends and the festive board,
   And wandered by moonlight pale.

They tell how he haunted the fatal shade
   Where the mourner first won his proud heart ;
How he softened the scorn of the pitying maid,
   And stole on her soul by his art.

They tell how 'twas rumoured Sir Eldred had died
   In a foreign and barbarous land ;
How her new lover soothed her and flattered her
      pride,
   Till she promised to yield him her hand.

On the eve of the bridal, on courser white,
   He stopped at fair Leonore's bower,
And urged her to fly by the pale moonlight,
   For danger was hovering o'er.

He set her in haste on his snowy white steed,
   And flung o'er her his mantle of blue ;

The tangled wood stayed not their perilous speed,
 And o'er mountain and valley they flew.

He was cased in armour, his vizor was down,
 But she gazed on his terrible eye;
Its language was dark, she shrank from its frown,
 But she trembled to ask him for why.

In silence they went, till the terrified maid
 Asked, trembling. how far they must ride?
" A priest in yon abbey is waiting," he said,
 " My fair one, to make thee my bride."

By a newly dug grave fair Leonore saw
 A priest stand with uncovered head;
And he read, with a voice of tremulous awe,
 The service which honours the dead.

And round, there stood a mourning train,
 All clad in the garb of woe:
And they were chanting the requiem strain
 In cadences mournful and low.

Her lover looked on with a bitter smile,
 'Twas a fearful smile to see;
" Sir Priest, thou must rest from that work awhile.
 To marry my true love and me."

Fair Leonore turned as she heard him speak,
 And aside his dark mantle he threw;

                                           c

His vizor was raised, she uttered a shriek,
  For the face of Sir Eldred she knew.

On his helmet was waving a long dark tress,
  With a ringlet of silvery grey ;
And white with the raven-black plume of his crest,
  A garland of hawthorn did play.

" Come, let me adorn thee as fitting my bride,"
  In a deep hollow murmur he said,
As he tore the white wreath from his helmet's pride,
  And twined it round Leonore's head.

Then he drew the pale maid to the wide yawning
      grave,
  And pointed with shadowy hand ;
" There lies thy Sir Eldred, the faithful and brave,
  Basely slain by his rival's command.

" For seven long moons has my murdered form
  In a barbarous region been laid,
Unhonoured and bare to the pitiless storm,
  In the deep wood's guilty shade.

" The lord of the valley may howl in despair,
  Thou hast vowed and thou yet shall be mine ;
Come, join thy pale bridegroom in regions of air,
  His spirit shall mingle with thine."

She sank in the grave on the dead man's breast,
   That bosom so still and so cold ;
But his bloodless arms were round her prest,
   And he held her in icy fold.

No human might could those arms unclasp,
   Though many a prayer was said ;
But soon as she sank in that death-cold grasp,
   Fair Leonore's spirit had fled.

Now the spectre knight, on his shadowy steed,
   And his lady by moonlight pale,
Are seen, while he flies, with incredible speed,
   To chase the false lord of the vale.

THE FORSAKEN.

Why should I bind my hair with flowers,
　Or teach my braided locks to shine?
The eyes they pleased in happier hours,
　Now gaze on brighter locks than mine.

Away with all this idle show,
　It mocks me with unfitting bloom;
These wreaths were on my mournful brow,
　As roses scattered o'er a tomb.

I'd have a sombre garland made,
　Dark cypress and funereal yew;
This brow of sadness I would shade
　With something of congenial hue.

Why should I join the festive throng,
　Where mirthful tones my peace annoy?
Ah! what to me is dance or song?
　They cannot wake a kindred joy.

And where are music's soothing powers ?
 I only hear in that soft swell
The requiem of departed hours,
 The dirge of pleasures loved too well.

I threw me by the ocean's side,
 And watched the restless billows roll ;
The sullen murmur of the tide
 Made music fitted to my soul.

Upon the shore, with careful hand,
 I traced the lines my fancy gave ;
And marked how soon the yielding sand
 Resigned them to the sweeping wave.

And thus I said, *Man's* fickle mind
 Awhile some treasured form may bear,
But time steals o'er, nor leaves behind
 A trace of fond impression there.

IMPROMPTU.

Bettina, though the flow'ry wreath,
  Which thy kind hand for me had twined,
Long since hath faded unto death,
  Breathed its last odour on the wind ;
Yet cease to mourn its transient doom,
  For memory's inmost cell doth bear
The treasured gift, and bids it bloom
  In renovated beauty there.

TO THE WESTWOOD OAK.

THE Druid bard of other days would look
  Upon thy form with reverence less profound
Than I behold thee, thou majestic oak!
  Stretch thy wide shadow o'er this circling mound.

May the axe spare thy venerable age,
  Idly around thee may fierce Eurus blow,
Harmless above thy head the tempest rage,
  Nor rend one honour from thy sacred brow.

My heart's recording book thy trunk shall be,
  Each treasured name that faithful page shall bear,
Time of thy youthful grace may ravage thee,
  Yet those dear names unharmed shall flourish there.

The woodbine's wreaths thy branches shall adorn,
  And breathe their incense round thy favoured seat:
For oft within that circle hast thou drawn
  The cheerful, friendly band I love to meet.

When yon forsaken roof is theirs no more,
    When in those walls no form beloved I spy,
No ready step to meet me at the door,
    And speak my welcome with the beaming eye.

Oh! when those gates are coldly closed on me,
    When each deserted room looks blank and bare,
Thou'lt stretch thy verdant arms, dear faithful tree,
    I yet may find a friendly shelter there.

And while beneath thy canopy I rest,
    And feed my sorrows with the sad survey,
Dreams of the past shall triumph o'er my breast,
    Peopling thy shade with beings far away.

Fancy shall bid the friendly group arise
    That erst assembled in thy magic bound;
On me shall beam the light of absent eyes,
    And distant voices bless me with their sound.

The rugged cliff, the wave's unruffled blue,
    The little light-winged skiff that glides beneath
The scattered farms, the grove of various hue,
    The dark plantation, the uncultured heath ;

The smoke, slow rising from the sheltered vale,
    Where lurks the shepherd's peaceful cot unseen ;
The hill bold swelling, the retiring dale,
    The waving corn fields and the meadows green.

Each object witnessed from this wild retreat
  Shall speak of brighter hours, too bright to last ;
Hours, which my loved companions made so sweet,
  Sweet hours ! ah, wherefore should ye fly so fast ?

Where'er I roam, however changed my lot,
  From my true heart these scenes shall never fade;
Affection still shall hover o'er the spot,
  And memory hallow each familiar shade.

THE FORCED SMILE.

'Tis hard to force that rayless smile,
　　That gives no lustre to the eye,
Which plays upon the lip awhile,
　　But brings the cheek no warmer dye.
It is as though a meteor's gleam
　　Just tinged a cloud with sudden light,
Just glanced upon a frozen stream,
　　Then fled, and left no traces bright.
The dark cloud brightened as it passed,
　　The streamlet caught its transient ray ;
But ah ! no warmth the meteor cast,
　　No roseate colours tracked its way

TO THE LAST ROSE.

Thou lingering flower of summer's bloom,
   What dost thou here?
Are not thy sisters in their tomb?
Would'st thou survive the general doom,
   The dying year?

Strange! now from Autumn's sadd'ning brow
   Drops the pale wreath;
Thy cheek with tints so warm should glow,
Thy bosom breathe such fragrance now
   O'er scenes of death.

Alas! thou lone, thou lovely flower,
   I view in thee
An emblem of the last sweet hour
Of many, that for evermore
   Have passed from me.

The summer rose, my hours of joy
    Together came ;
I've seen those hours and roses die,
And thou, fair flower, ere long must lie
    Withering with them.

But though thy glowing hues decay,
    We will not part ;
And though the last hour speeds away.
Yet its sweet mem'ry ne'er shall stray
    From this sad heart.

I'll cherish thee, thou rosebud fair,
    When beauty's flown ;
Thy every petal hoard with care,
And each shall some fond record bear
    Of moments gone.

From scenes and friends beloved so well,
    'Tis hard to sever ;
'Tis sweet on past delights to dwell,
'Tis sad when Reason comes to tell
    They're past for ever !

TO THE STARS.

Ye silent watchers of the night,
  That sentinel the solemn sky !
Whence is that pure and holy light,
  That beams from every starry eye ?

Fain would I deem that living flame
  The pledge divine of peace and love ;
Symbol of th' Eternal Name,
  Traced in bright characters above.

Downward ye look with tranquil gaze,
  On human woe and crime and strife,
Still moving in harmonious maze,
  Above the storms of mortal life.

There's beauty in the gladsome earth,
  There's grandeur in the pathless sea !
And every form of nature's birth
  Speaks matchless skill and bounty free.

But in yon lofty starlit dome,
  So solemn, holy, and sublime,
The *winged* soul beholds its home,
  And soars beyond the bounds of time.

Beautiful stars! was it for nought
  Your forms in radiant orbs were cast ?
No—but to wake the pious thought,
  that light and truth shall rule at last.

Mysterious worlds! still daring man,
  With soaring mind, will seek in vain
To solve the universal plan,
  Till God vouchsafe to make it plain.

IMPROMPTU.

WRITTEN ON THE SAND.

WHILE kneeling on the golden sand,
With beating heart and trembling hand,
  The name beloved I trace;
The wave which next comes sweeping o'er,
May, ere it leaves the pebbly shore,
  The characters erase.

But in my bosom's inmost cell
That name is traced too deep, too well,
  By aught to be removed;
The tide of years may onward roll,
But never from my faithful soul
  Shall sweep that name beloved.

JANUARY 1st, 1837.

'Tis midnight; and hark! on the clear cold air,
   There pealeth a sound that awakens my heart,
Forgotten scenes to my couch repair,
   And buried forms into beings start.

There is magical power in your voices, ye bells,
   To call up the ghosts of the sepulchred past;
My spirit replies to your musical spells,
   While their changing shadows fond memories
      cast.

Childhood hath fled like a dream away,
   With its sportive wiles and its short-lived flowers;
And youth hath passed as an April day,
   With its buds of promise and gilded showers.

The days of my sunny prime are gone,
   And some of its roses I thought were my own,
But the blooming petals dropped one by one,
   And I grasped but the thorny stem alone.

Autumn is come with its chastened glow,
  And its mellowed fruits for a wintry store ;
But the yellow leaf whirls from the topmost bough,
  And the blooms of summer are mine no more.

I see in the distance, with stealthy pace,
  Stern Winter advancing, begirt with his snows :
When his chill touch withers the last lingering
    grace,
  And scatters hoar frosts o'er my care-furrowed
    brows,
  Ah where shall I seek for my lost summer rose ?

Oh Sharon's sweet rose! I have found thee now,
  Thou hast taught me the worth of that blossom-
    less stem ;
Hence thy thorny chaplet I bind on my brow,
  And scorn a less glorious diadem.

THE DEPARTURE OF THE SWALLOWS.

Birds of the restless, wandering wing,
Joyous companions of the Spring!
   Heralds of Summer's rosy hours,
Stay—stay awhile your parting flight,
As yet the Autumn noon is bright,
   And beauty lingers with the flowers.

Your insect prey still haunts the stream,
Still dances in the western beam,
   The thrush yet pours his gushing lay;
The woodland bowers are densely green,
No faded yellow leaf is seen,
   Then wherefore would ye speed away?

Like Angel messengers, ye bring
Glad tidings from th' Eternal King,
   Of glorious summer's blessed birth
Your low sweet song proclaims the reign,
Of peace and love restored again,
   To renovate the gladdened earth.

Oh tarry yet awhile with me,
I cannot bear to part from ye,
  Sweet guests of Summer's radiant day ;
With ye all lovely things appear,
That charm the eye, enchant the ear,
  And with ye they will pass away.

Yet go—seek some more genial clime,
Full well ye know th' appointed time,
  Ye faithful followers of the Sun ;
Still his illumined track pursue,
Still keep his worshipped beam in view,
  And wintry cold and darkness shun.

Farewell, farewell ! but ere we part,
I take the lesson to my heart,
  Nor wish in this cold world to stay ;
Still onward, with obedient flight,
Spread my glad wings for scenes more bright,
  Where God sheds one eternal day.

THE DESOLATE HEART.

Who knoweth the pang of the desolate heart ?
She who hath toiled through the weary day
With household cares for one that's away,
Who hath bent o'er the pillow of infantine sleep,
And then in her loneliness turneth to weep,
And count the dull hours till her Lord's return,
And watch how the fast waning tapers burn,
At each passing sound she starts from her seat,
And her pulses throb with a quicker beat,
For she fancies the clang of his courser's feet,
Then hopelessly sighs as the cock's shrill tone
Warns her to creep to her couch alone,
Where she watcheth and prayeth for him the while,
Who hath left her side for a wanton's smile—
Neglected wife! whoever thou art,
Thou knowest the pang of the desolate heart !

Who knoweth the pang of the desolate heart ?

She who hath numbered her spring's young hours,
And plucked the last wreath of her summer's bright
    flowers,
In her maiden bower she sitteth alone,
Musing o'er loves and o'er friendships flown,
And broods on the past till the teardrops start—
She knoweth the pang of the desolate heart!

Who knoweth the pang of the desolate heart?
He who, enthroned in His glory above,
Came down from the regions of light and love,
(Where hosts of bright angels awaited his call,)
To suffer for man on this sin-darkened ball,
Alone, mid the thousands His bounty had fed,
Creation's dread Lord, had no place for his head.
Betrayed, denied, " forsaken and fled,"
By those who had shared in his daily bread,
He who endured in that last dark hour
" The sting of death" in its fiercest power,
Which wrung from His bosom that agonized cry,
" My God, why hast thou forsaken me," why?
Now enthroned in His glory above,
He looks from the region of light and love ;
He hath borne all thy sorrows, He taketh thy part,
He knoweth and healeth the desolate heart.

AUTUMN FLOWERS.

I LOVE the fair young buds of spring,
  And the tender green of the vernal bowers,
When the light breeze bears on his gossamer wing
  The odorous breath of the violet flowers.

When the primrose peeps from the mossy nook,
  And the pearly hawthorn scents the air,
And the sweet brier hangs o'er the glassy brook,
  And blushes to find her cheek so fair.

But the sweet young spring has a changeful brow,
  And the green buds shrink from her frowning
      face,
E'en the venturous hyacinth crouches low,
  And wraps her bells in their silken case.

I love the hour when summer glows,
  When the bee and the butterfly revel in bloom,
When Zephyr sports with the laughing rose,
  And pants with his burden of rich perfume.

—

But the green moss pales on the streamlet's brink,
  When the landscape is wrapt in a fiery haze;
And the brightest blossom will fade and shrink,
  When the sun looks down with too bold a gaze.

But autumn flowers, bright autumn flowers!
  The charm of your beauty is freshness and glow;
Ye are smiling on, when from fading bowers
  The yellow leaf whirls from the storm-shaken
    bough.

Ye laugh in the sunshine, ye dance in the gale,
  Ye shake from your tresses the chill dews of
    night,
Ye gaze undismayed when the tempests assail,
  And glow mid the darkness as creatures of light.

As the long-tried friends of our youth ye stay,
  When the gauds of summer have spent their
    bloom,
Like Angel spirits to bless our way,
  And brighten our path to the wintry tomb.

A SKETCH,

DRAWN FROM LIFE BY THE SEA-SHORE.

THE FISHER'S WIFE.

She stood and watched him from the beetling brow
Of the tall cliff, and listened with fond ear,
As, busied at his wonted task to fit
His little light-winged skiff for the blue wave,
He whistled sprightly notes, his heart's wild music,
Sweeter to her, that untaught melody,
Than all the varied strains of laboured art.
It touched her simple bosom's answering chords,
And told her of a thousand smiling things,
Homeborn delights, endearing fireside joys,
When resting from his daily toil, at eve,
With her he sat, and still with gentle words
And sunny looks repaid her watchful cares.
A laughing boy she clasps in her fond arms,
And oft she breathes the fondly cherished name
Of " Father," to the pleased and playful child,
That points its dimpled hand to mark the spot,
The well-known spot, where, on the pebbly shore,

He spreads his nets and stretches the white sail.
His gallant little skiff, the well-earned meed
Of his industrious hours, with honest pride
He views, and now his cheerful shout is heard,
And instant bounding from the rugged side
Of the steep cliff, his sturdy mates obey
The wonted signal, and their captain's pride
Dances already on the heaving wave.
He turns to gaze upon his happy home,
And that fair form which crowned his household bliss
Met his pleased eye; and that dear mutual joy,
That sportive cherub with its rose-tinged cheek,
Its sunny ringlets, and blue laughing eyes,
Spell-bind his steps, how can he leave the shore,
While that sweet vision lures him to return?
With rapid stride he rushes up the steep,
And once more clasps his treasures to his heart
With many a fond caress and loving pledge;
Then joins his waiting comrades, springs on board,
And gives his swelling sail to the light breeze.
I saw that gentle woman wipe the tears
That slowly gathered in her deep blue eye;
They came unbidden, for she was not sad;
They were the tender tribute of her love
To him upon whose bosom she had leaned
The minutes past, and he was gone to toil

A few brief hours for those he cherished most.
No coward fears were trembling in her heart,
She was a *hero's* wife, and that still wave,
On which her husband's little pinnace sat,
Like a blue halcyon calmly floating there,
That azure mirror, could not shock her soul
With presages of dread, for she had seen
That little pinnace, as a bird of storm
Careering proudly o'er the crested waves,
Dipping her white wing in the wreathed foam,
And braving all the fury of the blast—
E'en in those hours a calm and holy trust
Stilled the wild fears that throbbed her woman's
          heart.
Now, all was tranquil, bright, and beautiful,
And those soft drops which gemmed her fringed lids
Fell on her cheek as dew upon the flowers,
Brightening the roseate bloom that mantled there :
Her earnest eye still followed the white sail,
And the gay pennon streaming on the breeze,
Till the bold jutting cliff, with envious point,
Shut from her view the form beloved, and then
Slowly she turned to seek her cottage home,
And wing with household cares the lagging hours.
Past was the morn's fair prime—again I saw
That youthful mother and that sportive child

O'erlooking the wide sea : a change came o'er
Its tranquil bosom—dark'ning the blue wave.
The wind was busy with her fluttering robes,
And rudely scattered her dark silken hair ;
And her fair boy clung closer to her breast.
Black massive clouds hung like a mournful pall
Over the deep, which the fierce howling blast
Lashed into fury, and each yawning wave
Shewed "like the grave of some devoted bark."
The aged seamen gather on the cliff,
And watch the progress of the awful storm.
Here, a fond mother, *there*, an anxious wife
Paces with restless step and straining eye ;
While many a dismal tale of gone-by storms,
Of foundering vessels and their hapless crew,
Of childless mothers and of widowed wives ;
Fill with foreboding fears that trembling group.
There were but *two*, whose bosoms were not wild
With dread of ill.   *One* clapped his little hands,
And laughed for joy to see the billows toss
Their snowy manes on high, and the wild winds
Chase the light frothy globes along the strand.
The *other*, with a calm and steady gaze,
Surveyed the elemental strife, her heart
Fast anchored on the " Rock of ages," rode
E'en like a gallant ship above the storm,

A hope sublime and holy smoothed her brow,
A patient trust subdued her natural dread,
And still she sought with cheering words to soothe
The clamorous terrors of the gathered crowd,
As if upon that black, perturbed sea
Her own heart's treasure had not been embarked.
So calm her bearing showed, that those unskilled
To read the heart's deep mysteries, might deem
Hers cold and passionless, but He who stilled
Her spirit's tempest, knew that deeper love
Ne'er dwelt in woman's breast than throbbed in hers.
I saw her hastening to her lowly home,
To trim the hearth, and rouse the cheerful blaze,
To greet her storm-drenched mariner's return.
And did he then return ?—the cottage door
Was yet unclosed when a rejoicing shout
Proclaimed a sail! a sail! With breathless haste
She flies—regains the cliff, and knows full well
The gallant bearing of that fairy barque,
Though her dismantled mast stooped to the deep,
And her storm-tattered sail clung idly there.
On, on she dashes through the angry surf,
And lands in safety her adventurous crew.
A cry of transport bursts from Mary's lips,
And the next moment sees the happy wife
Shedding sweet tears upon her husband's breast.

FAREWELL TO THE OLD YEAR, 1852.

There are, who sunk in careless sleep
  Heed not, old year, thy passing knell;
Fain would I solemn vigil keep,
  To bid thee, dying friend, farewell.

I would not have thee fleet away,
  Albeit thou'st cost me many a tear,
Without *one* tributary lay,
  One willow wreath to deck thy bier.

If ever in thy onward way
  Thy hand for me a garland strung,
Rude storm-winds have forbid its stay,
  And far away the sweet gift flung.

The day hath had a frowning close,
  Which met me with a smile at dawn;
And if, perchance, I've plucked a rose,
  My hand hath surely felt the thorn.

Farewell, harsh teacher as thou art,
  Thou shalt not from my memory flee ;
Thou leavest me with a chastened heart,
  And therefore will I honor thee.

REMINISCENCES.

We trod together our flowery path
  In the sunny days of youth ;
We loved, as young hearts only love,
  With pure confiding truth.

Thou just escaped from school-day thrall,
  And *I* in girlhood's bloom,
Met in my sire's ancestral hall,
  My childhood's happy home.

What simple pleasures winged the hours
  Within our calm retreat,
Our books, our pencils, music, flowers,
  Together shared, how sweet !

Oft in the sultry hours of noon,
  We trod the shadowy dell,
Or 'neath the "glimpses of the moon,"
  We sought the hermit's cell.

Still paused we by the streamlet's brink,
  To watch the sparkling sheen,
And see the willows stoop to drink,
  Which formed our leafy screen.

Our star of life shone clear and bright,
  No shadows dimmed its ray;
We felt no chill, we feared no blight,
  For all looked fair and gay.

But time stole on, and thou must climb
  Ambition's giddy steep,
And spend afar thy manhood's prime,
  And I be left to weep.

Our farewell pledge was violet flowers,
  No vows dwelt on our tongue,
No promise bound our parting hours,
  For *these* we were too young.

Haply within our hearts might rise
  Hopes unexpressed, but fair;
We looked into each other's eyes,
  And read our future there.

Years passed away, and thou hadst won
  The deathless wreath of fame,
And first upon the victor's scroll
  Appeared thy lofty name.

Methinks I see thy stately form,
   And flashing eye of pride,
When glorious from the battle's storm
   Thou camest to claim thy bride.

Oh! with what joy did we retrace
   The paths our childhood trod:
We loved and praised fair Nature's face;
   But we forgot her God.

With warbling birds and wild flowers' bloom,
   And rippling streamlets clear,
We saw an Eden in our home,
   Nor deemed the serpent near.

Our air-built dome, too frail to last,
   Based on the shifting sand,
By life's first dreadful storm o'ercast,
   Lay wrecked upon the strand.

My sire, who once thy suit denied,
   Would now that suit approve;
But ah! to feed vindictive pride,
   Thine, sacrificed our love.

Oh! scalding are the tears that start
   When life's young dream hath fled,
They well, like life-blood from the heart,
   And leave it seared and dead.

E.

The purpose of thy life o'erthrown,
    Thy dream of joy was past,
My ardent heart was turned to stone;
    Then frenzy came at last.

Whilst thou the wine-cup madly drained
    To drown thy careless grief,
A dreary blank to me remained,
    And then, there came relief.

But honour calls, and thou must go
    To India's burning shore,
To win fresh laurels for thy brow,
    And thus we met no more.

And though with one who sought me long,
    I found a peaceful home,
And gave to him my grateful love,
    'Twas love without its bloom.

Thou'rt wandering yet in distant lands,
    And *I*, a widowed wife,
Count wearily my ebbing sands;
    Ah me! and is this life?

Hush! murmuring heart! nor seek *alone*
    The ills of life to bear;
Lay at the Cross thy burden down, .
    Thou'lt find thy solace there.

SONNET.

THE NAMELESS GRAVE.

Nor sculptured marble canopies the head
So coldly pillowed there, nor rustic stone
Records the name of that departed one.
The time-worn ruin from th' unhallowed tread
Defends it; but that low and cheerless bed
No sun-glow brightens, a wan light alone
Gilds the grey arches, when the full-orbed moon
Flings shadowy mysteries o'er the nameless dead.
No verdure smiles on that neglected sod.
But wreaths of mournful ivy clasp the mound,
And a young grove of elders gather round
As if to watch o'er the unhonoured clod.
Sleeper! thy name is registered with God,
And thou shalt waken at the trumpet's sound.

STANZAS.

I WANDERED by the ocean side,
  And watched the billows ceaseless roll ;
The solemn murmur of the tide
  Made music suited to my soul ;
Each strong emotion of the breast
Was sweetly calmed and hushed to rest.

I traced upon the yellow strand
  The names that fond remembrance gave,
And marked how soon the treacherous sand
  Would yield them to the sweeping wave ;
Onward it rolls, and now the shore
Retains those cherished names no more.

I thought on days long passed away,
  On love's warm hopes and friendship's glow ;
Fair flowers ! that mocked my youthful day,
  Where is your flattering beauty now ?
Full many a bud I've lived to see
Wither or bloom no more for me.

Hearts are grown cold that lately seemed
　To leap with joy at my advance,
And eyes that once with fondness beamed,
　Now turn a cold, averted glance;
These things have cost me many a groan,
But now their bitterness is gone!

Change is inscribed on all below,
　Yea, death in everything I see;
Then why should earth attract thee so,
　My heart? what is this earth to thee?
Its cares and joys, its hopes and fears,
All vanish when thy Lord appears.

Thou canst not rest, poor fluttering thing,
　The swelling waves forbid thy stay;
Still must thou stretch thy feeble wing,
　Still onward fly thy weary way;
Thou, trembling Dove! shalt find no rest
Save in the ark, thy Saviour's breast.

TO ———.

YEARS have rolled on, and we have met,
　But not as we were wont to meet;
Coldly we bade farewell, and yet,
As though we could not quite forget
　When intercourse was free and sweet.

And is it thus we meet and part,
　My early friend, and art thou gone?
Thy love still twines around my heart;
These tears attest how dear thou art;
　I've only loved thee less than *One!*

One who hath shed his blood for me,
　And claims me to be all His own;
One who hath set my spirit free
From earth's delusive vanity,
　And bids me seek a Heavenly crown.

That *One* e'en more than thee I prize,
　And for His sake thy loss can bear;
Then let us part! yet to yon skies
Thy friend will raise her suppliant eyes,
　And pray that she may meet thee there.

TO ILLUSTRATE
A PAINTING OF TWO FROGS SITTING
UNDER A MUSHROOM.

Two frogs which had spent their whole lives in a fen,
Remote from the dwellings of civilised men,
Beginning to find such seclusion a bore,
Determined to quit, and set out on a tour;
So a council was held by the whole croaking nation
To discuss the great subject of frog-emigration,
As a means of correcting confined education.
The point was well argued on one side the question,
When a sage-looking frog rose to make a suggestion.
" We have dwelt," said the elder, " in comfort and
            ease,
In this pool, whence we pop out or in as we please,
And our ancestors here lived contented and free,
For no nation on earth can be freer than we.
Should we venture to stray from this peaceful retreat,
Who knows what disasters and toils we may meet?
My mind is, that every well-judging frog
Be content where he is, and still stick to the bog."

Th' assembly was struck with this splendid oration,
And croaked in full chorus their just approbation.
So the council broke up and abandoned the scheme,
Save the two restless spirits that started the theme.
Said Croaker, " This antediluvian lore
Comes well from a doting old frog of fourscore.
But Froglings of spirit should scorn such weak
      trash ;
For me, I'm determined to made a bold dash.
The moon is just up, it is very fine weather,
So make up your mind, and let's hop off together."
" Agreed, but be silent, for fear of detection ;
If our parents awake, they will raise an objection."
So off went the friends quite light-hearted and gay,
And talked of the wonders they met by the way ;
They travelled all night by the light of the moon,
And cleared the morass just before it was noon.
The day was so sultry, that *Sprawly* was fain
To pause and just stretch his long shanks on the
      plain,
And they *both* thought with secret regret on the
      pool
Where their kindred were basking so charmingly
      cool ;
Said Croaker, " I spy a delicious retreat,
Yon mushroom will shelter us both from the heat ;"

So they squatted beneath, and so ample its spread,
That it formed quite a canopy over each head ;
They sat on their haunches and looked just as grand,
As if they were monarchs of Faëry land.
Quoth Croaker, " How travel enlarges the mind !
And the appetite too, I'm beginning to find."
Said Sprawly, " Let's peep out for something to eat,
A breakfast were now a delectable treat. "
" Hush ! hush !" whispered Croaker, "don't make
        such a fuss,
Or yon monstrous bird will make breakfast of us."
A Heron just flapped his broad wings o'er the waste,
So the comrades sneaked back to their shelter in
        haste,
And skulked till the scream died away on the blast,
But popped out as soon as the danger was past ;
And though somewhat feeble, resuming their route,
Returned to the theme they were talking about.
Said Croaker, " I own I am fired with ambition
To make the *grand tour*, as befits my condition.
A Frogling of rank should know something of life,
Before he sits down with his children and wife ;
My pedigree dates from the reign of ' King Log,'
And your ancestor was a most valorous Frog."
" Yes, truly," said Sprawley, " the deeds of my sire
Were worthy the great Grecian Bard to inspire,

Who sang their exploits on his heroic lyre ;
But methinks I would barter my ancestral fame
For a good meal of slugs now, for what's in a name
When the stomach is empty, and craving for food?
So pray let us try to find something that's good."
They hopped up a hillock, and saw with delight
A broad sheet of water so cooling and bright ;
But Sprawly shrank back from some objects he saw
Skimming over its surface, and silenced his craw.
Said Croaker, " Friend Sprawl, you know nothing,
  I see,
Be tranquil and leave our safe convoy to me ;
Those monsters you speak of, which make such bold
  dips,
Are snug floating houses, by mankind called ships ;
Let us hop to the water, and since we need rest,
We will call for a boat and take passage to Brest."
So his friend taking courage hopped on by his side,
And they joyfully bathed their tired limbs in the
  tide ;
But poor Croaker's *Flotilla* soon sailed on their track,
And gobbled up both with a satisfied *quack*.—
Thus folly and pride lured these frogs to their
  doom ;
So youngsters beware of a passion to roam,
Be content in your youth to learn wisdom at home.

RECIPE FOR A SCENT JAR.

Go to thy garden's perfumed bowers,
When Spring awakes the laughing flowers,
Cull the sweet blossoms, ere they fade,
Of violets lurking in the shade,
Pale primroses that love to dwell
On shady bank or weeping dell,
Cowslips that lure with honied breath
The wild bee rover from the heath ;
Aspiring lilacs which exhale
Arabian spices on the gale;
The fair Syringa's breathing flowers,
That emulate Ausonia's bowers,
And when the ripening summer glows,
Snatch from her breast the peerless rose.
Its blushing petals freely shower,
Amid the fair and fragrant store,
With jasmine blossoms silvery white,
Like stars upon the brow of night.

Go where the clustering woodbines twine,
Where blushes the wild eglantine,
Where mignonette sweet breath exhales,
And lavender the sense regales;
Where wall-flowers grateful odour fling,
And stocks allure each insect wing.
Take them while yet their radiant eyes
Gaze on the fair unclouded skies;
Soon as their worshipped sun appears,
To kiss away the morning's tears.
Now let a vase of ample size
Receive the beauteous floral prize,
Then strew o'er all, with liberal hand,
The spicy spoils of India's land,
But most the *snowy mineral** shower,
That wondrous life-preserving power;
So in the hours of wintry gloom
Shall summer's breath pervade the room;
When the bright sun has chased the dew,
Each morn the pleasing task renew,
Till the sweet blooming time is o'er,
Or the full vase can hold no more.

* Bay salt.

TO THE BEE.

On welcome to my noontide seat,
  Thou child of sunbeams wild and free !
That lov'st to woo each floral sweet,
  Gay wanderer, how I envy thee !

A honied load is all thy care,
  Thy roughest path mid perfumed bowers,
Thy hardest toil to skim the air,
  And roam o'er beds of fairest flowers.

Stay—stay awhile thy restless wing,
  And let me still thy murmur hear ;
That murmur is the voice of spring,
  Oh! it is music to my ear.

A thousand odours with that sound
  Come floating on the western breeze,
A thousand blooms are scattered round,
  And buds of promise gem the trees.

Oh happy bee! what bliss is thine,
  For thee the blushing queen is born,
Securely on her breast recline,
  For thee she points no treacherous thorn.

I see thee flit o'er sunny beds,
  To kiss the violet's eye of blue ;
I see thee bend the primrose heads,
  To sip that flower's delicious dew.

Now clinging to a cowslip's bell,
  Now in a jonquil's bosom laid ;
Now in a woodbine's fragrant cell,
  Where thy loved sunbeams kindly played.

Go seek the wall with garlands drest,
  Where spreads the peach her liberal bloom ;
There flit about, profusely blest,
  Then bear thy golden treasure home.

Oh welcome to my noontide seat,
  Thou child of sunbeams wild and free,
That lov'st to woo each floral sweet,
  Gay wanderer! how I envy thee!

ON READING SOME LINES IN CENSURE OF THE LATE LORD BYRON.

AND is that master-spirit fled?
And bowed to earth that lofty head,
And mute that tongue's imperious tone,
And sunk that brow's dark withering frown,
And quenched that eye's excursive glance,
Which ranged Creation's wide expanse?
That eye where frenzied genius shone,
Kindling whate'er it glanced upon,
As when the storm's dark shadowy wing
Awakes the wind harp's answering string,
So his inspiring numbers came,
Thrilling each chord of feeling's frame,
Till that wild music's influence stole
Like a strong passion on the soul.
Ye blighters of his fame! forbear!
Would ye the mouldering relics tear

From earth's kind sheltering breast, and tread
With reckless footsteps on the dead ?
Think ye the partner of his vows,
Or that "lone scion of his house,"
Will joy to find reproach and shame
Follow the memory of that name ?
Will not their generous feelings spurn
The rude disturbers of his urn ?
Will not their gentle bosoms bleed,
And shudder at such heartless deed ?
Oh ! let the weeping marble hide
All that was *not* his country's pride.
Whate'er he did, or spake or wrote,
That charity would wish forgot,
Oh breathe it not ! let silence steep
Its memory in oblivious sleep.
Perhaps in that last solemn hour,
When earth's delusions charmed no more,
And swiftly from his glazing eye
Rolled off each shadowy vanity,
That erring spirit "knew the rod,"
And owned and blest the Christian's God.
The secrets of that hour are known
To that just God, and Him alone,
And shall be till that awful day
When heaven and earth shall pass away !

Proud genius may a lesson find,
From the sad wreck of that vast mind ;
That mighty mind whose giant grasp
Could learning's ponderous tomes unclasp ;
That powerful mind whose noontide blaze
Dimmed all contemporary rays ;
That powerful mind could not discern
What humbler Heav'n-taught spirits learn.
Not all the light by science given,
Can guide man's wandering feet to Heaven.

SONNET

TO NIGHT.

On, night, I love thy dark and silent reign,
  When all the tedious din of life is o'er;
When the tired world sinks 'neath the charmèd
    power
  Of tranquillizing sleep, that chases pain
  From the sad sufferer's brow and crowds his brain
With images of joy, thine are the hours
When Fancy loves to twine her wreathèd flowers,
  Ah! let her not invoke thine aid in vain!
To me more lovely is thy ebon brow,
Though not a star thy diadem adorns,
To me more welcome than the orient glow,
When Phœbus flings his tresses on the thorn,
For thy waste silent hours escape control,
And spread the banquet to my hungry soul.

TO MY BROTHER, A. J., WITH FLOWERS.

I HAVE ransacked the beds, I have ravaged the
    bowers,
To find brother Ambrose the fairest of flowers,
To brighten his cell while their beauty shall last,
And to live on his canvas when life shall be past ;
But, alas for my boasting, I find, to my cost,
That the brightest and best have been nipped by
    Jack Frost.
The morning rose fair, and the noon-tide was bright,
The evening with blushes had ushered in night :
The stars shone out clear, and each sharp-pointed ray
Gave hints of the pranks Frost intended to play.
That demon of mischief already was near,
He peered from the moon with malevolent sneer ;
From his thin, shrivelled lips these stinging words
    came,
That chilled every blossom and thrilled through its
    frame.
" These minions of Flora, that cut such a dash,
That have smiled through each storm, and shook off
    each rain plash,

I will pelt with *white* stones, till I make them turn
　　pale,
And hang their pert heads, as the flower of the vale.
Rose de Chine, a relation of summer's bright Queen,
Still simpers and blushes, and tries to be seen.
But I'll pinch her soft cheek till I make it turn blue,
I'll teach her to mimic her cousin's bright hue!
Yon Fuchsia that towers with pride o'er the
　　ground,
Like a Chinese pagoda with bells hung around,
I will give such a shock from his toe to his crown
As shall change his rich crimson to dull tawny brown;
There is Lady Anemone decked out so bright,
With her splendid mantilla of scarlet and white,
But I'll tear it to tatters, and strew them around,
Till torn and dismantled she stands on the ground.
I'll blacken the fringe of her tall stately stem,
But in mockery leave her that rich diadem.
Polyanthus, the fop, has just perked up his head,
With his new velvet *wideawake,* yellow and red,
With his pale green *santoir,* and affected grimace ;
But I'll give him a squeeze that will blacken his face.
Primrose, his fair sister, meek child of the dale,
Already I've kissed her and made her turn pale ;
And I've sent the poor rustic to hide her young head
Within the green folds of her canopied bed.

There is Pansy, the dandy, in purple and gold,
Who changes so often his dress, I am told,
And affects to look young, though he's full twelve
      months old ;
But he looks in my face with so saucy a leer,
I will leave him alone till the end of the year.
And there is the Violet, pensive and sweet,
Just venturing forth from her leafy retreat ;
But I'll give a rebuff to that forward young thing,
That shall keep her in bed till the advent of spring.
And there is Forget-me-not living hard by,
Beginning to open her merry blue eye ;
But I'll frighten her so, to her couch she will creep,
And I'll give her a dose that shall lengthen her sleep.
Chrysanthemums flaunting in colours so gay,
With a touch of my finger shall wither away."
So spake the fell fiend, and his pestilent breath
Directly consigned his poor victims to death.
The rest of the train heard his menace with dread,
Each dropped timid tears and declined her fair head;
But some more robust survived the dark hour,
And shook their bright locks, and still laughed at
      his power.
So I send you my best, and I trust, gentle friend,
They'll arrive in good order and answer your end.

LINES WRITTEN IN THE LONG
WINTER OF 1814.

Ye leafless bowers, ye bloomless vales,
   Ye desolated plains !
Where Winter, breathing icy gales,
   Prolongs his tedious reign ;
Still through the dark, the joyless day,
Th' unvaried landscape I survey,
   I watch the fleecy shower ;
When will the tyrant quit the scene ?
Oh, when shall Spring, with smile serene,
   Your ravaged charms restore ?

Tell me, ye dim, snow-laden trees,
   That stretch your widowed arms ;
Will ye e'er flutter in the breeze,
   With renovated charms ?
Ye mournful shrubs ! will ye resume
Your vivid green, your various bloom,
   And flourish as before ?
Ye sleeping flowers, that hide the head
Beneath the cold earth's frozen bed,
   Will ye e'er blossom more ?

Ye choristers! that fill the grove
With anthems to Almighty love,
   Why are ye mute so long?
When will morn's herald pierce the sky,
And from that deep blue canopy
   Pour the full tide of song?

Ye fair, ye rainbow-tinted things!
That skim the pool with glancing wings,
   Or hide amid the bowers,
Ye lovers of the garden's bloom!
When will ye burst your silken tomb,
   And revel with the flowers?

Ye chartered pilferers of the gold
That Flora's jewelled coffers hold,
   Awake your bugle strain!
Ye countless winged sprites appear!
With hum and buzz enchant my ear,
   And tell of Summer's reign.

ALONE.

THE morning smiles—alone! alone!
   I gaze upon the sparkling sheen
Of diamond drops profusely sown
   O'er all that decks the rural scene.
My heart responds to Nature's voice;
Yet how can I *alone* rejoice?

I stray amid the woodland bowers,
   I hearken to the *wild* bird's lay,
I search each nook for hidden flowers,
   And treasure every blooming spray:
I praise their beauty with a groan,
For ah! I view them quite *alone!*

They greatly err, who say " the heart,
   When it has found communion high,
Can freely with its loved ones part,
   Nor needeth human sympathy."
Ah! He who strung its trembling chords,
Knoweth these are but dreamy words.

No rebel tears are these I shed,
  Father! to Thee I dare appeal!
While to thy stroke I bow my head,
  Thou will'st thy chastened one should feel.
I kiss the rod and own it just,
But my heart bleeds—and weep I must!

There is a high, mysterious life,
  Beyond the life that worldlings know ;
A peace unharmed by outer strife,
  While fainting nature owns the blow.
Fast falling tears may dim the eyes,
Yet soars the spirit to the skies !

FAREWELL TO 1858.

FAREWELL, farewell, old year! thou art the last
Dim, tarnished portion of the brighter past,
An iron link in that same golden chain
Of time, which I must never count again.
And I am free! free the wide world to range!
But to the captive, liberty seems strange.
I shrink and hide within my lonely cell,
And feel I loved my fetters but too well.
I am no more the stately fostering tree,
Beneath whose shade fair blossoms clustered free,
Around whose trunk would fondly clasp and twine
Green ivy wreaths, and loving sweet woodbine.
Through many a storm, that tree, more firmly bound,
Hath seen its leafy honours scattered round;
But when ungentle hands the rough bark tear,
The mantling wreaths flaunt wild, the wounded
     trunk stands bare!
The unclasped garlands for a moment droop,
But youthful plants instinct with life and hope,

With searching tendrils, float in air awhile,
Clasp the next prop, and then look up and smile.
But the dismantled tree, in lonely pain,
Bleeds at the core, and spreads its arms in vain!

"I LOATHE IT, I LOATHE IT. I WOULD NOT LIVE ALWAYS."

Oh, take me, Father! take me home!
  I have no portion here;
It irks my spirit yet to roam
  This desert lone and drear.

My best-beloved are gone before,
  And some who prized me well,
Their looks of love shall never more
  Brighten my lonely cell.

Oh bear me to my Mother Earth,
  Her arms shall wrap me round,
Till I shall spring to glorious birth,
  Waked by the trumpet's sound.

My panting soul with outstretched wings
  Awaits her call from thee,
And spurning earth's inferior things,
  She longeth to be free!

Free to dissolve in that pure breath
   From whence her being came,
Till Thou, who conquered sin and death,
   Reanimate this frame.

Oh blissful union! wondrous change!
   When shall fruition be?
When shall this glorious being range
   The fields of air with thee?

Lord, grant me patience to fulfil
   The measure of my span;
My only quest to know thy will,
   And carry forth thy plan.

A few brief years of toil and strife
   Perhaps for me remain,
Then shall I rise to endless life,
   And never weep again.

TO MY FOSTER-CHILD IN HEAVEN.

My child! what bitter tears I shed,
  While thou, in restless pain,
Wer't tossing on thy fevered bed,
And I not near, to bathe thy head,
  And cool thy throbbing brain.

I might not kiss thy burning brow,
  Nor clasp thy hand in mine,
Nor join the prayer God only heard,
Nor say the " fitly spoken word,"
  When consciousness was thine.

Oh! had'st thou heard my well-known tongue,
  Soothing thy transports wild,
Thy wakened love had backward sprung
To her who o'er thy pillow hung,
  When thou wert yet a child.

If e'er thy young warm heart hath owned
  A thought that made thee pine,
I might have probed thy bosom's wound,
And thou a safe relief have found,
  In trusting it to mine.

To me! who trained thy infant years,
  And watched thy girlhood's prime,
Read in thine eyes thy hopes, thy fears,
Fathomed thy wishes, dried thy tears,
  And taught thee truths sublime.

Ah, did'st thou not *one* record keep
  Upon thy wandering brain,
Of *her* who hushed thy baby sleep,
Of *her* whom thou hast left to weep
  In solitary pain?

And must I never more behold
  That beaming look of thine?
Those clustering curls of wavy gold,
Those earnest eyes, whose quick glance told
  The soul's rich sparkling mine?

Thy bounding step on Heathy Hill
  Shall never more be found,
Nor lingering by the mossy rill,
With ready pencil tracing still
  The graceful forms around.

My gifted one; in few I find,
  Whatever their degree,
Who, in the native powers of mind,
In works of skill, in taste refined,
  Can more than rival thee!

And thou, sweet girl! ere thou could'st climb
  Life's rugged steep, art gone!
Stopped in thy course in blooming prime,
While *I*, the wreck of grief and time,
  Drag my existence on!

Hush, murmuring heart! 'tis not for thee
  To question or repine.
Father in Heaven! 'tis thine to see
The fitness of thine own decree,
  Be meek submission mine!

A few brief years, and these sad eyes
  Will sleep their last long night;
Then my freed soul will upward rise,
Meet its lost treasure in the skies.
  And dwell with her in light!

"SHE IS NOT DEAD, BUT SLEEPETH."

SHE sleeps, but not as once she slept,
  When feverish cares perturbed her breast ;
Then, on a couch of down she wept,
And oft with pain sad vigil kept.
  She sleeps ! and nought can break her rest.

She sleeps, the green sod wraps her round,
  And coldly pillowed is her head ;
But oh ! her sleep is sweet and sound,
No storm can shake that deep profound.
  No cares disturb that narrow bed.

What though the Form we loved so well
  Must mingle soon with kindred dust :
Angels shall guard the lowly cell
Wherein those crumbling ashes dwell.
  Till power Divine redeem the trust.

That precious seed shall ne'er decay,
   'Tis sown in hope, 'tis watched with care,
Till it shall rise on that great day,
When God shall wake the slumbering clay,
   And clothe it with a form more fair.

We will not weep as some may weep,
   Whose hope expires with closing earth;
May we like her " in Jesus sleep,"
" In sure and certain hope" to reap
   The glories of our Heavenly birth.

Now, let us raise our mournful eyes,
   And trace the spirit freed from clay;
Lo! she hath won the Heavenly prize!
She meets her Lord in Paradise,
   And He hath wiped her tears away!

RETROSPECTION.

In early day, when life was young,
　When hopes were unsuspected wiles,
When Pleasure like a syren sung,
　And wore a radiant mask of smiles—

I knew not that enchanting light
　Was but the meteor's transient glare,
That shoots athwart the vault of night,
　But leaves no trace of brightness there.

But ere the morn of life was past,
　Pale sorrow dimmed each specious ray;
And disappointment's withering blast
　Whirled the sweet flowers of Hope away.

Awhile I wept my joys o'erthrown,
　But tears soon fail in youthful eyes,
And youthful hearts, unwont to groan,
　From sorrow's touch elastic rise.

G 2

I gave to earth my heart again,
  New friendships formed, new pleasures planned;
I leaned on " broken reeds," and then
  Grieved that they pierced my trusting hand.

When deeper woes obscured my day,
  When all my cherished hopes had fled,
The Eye of Mercy watched my way,
  The Arm of Might my footsteps led.

Oh! when I deemed myself alone,
  That Arm sustained my sinking form;
When every earthly stay was gone,
  I sought a refuge from the storm.

I wandered in this waste of woe,
  And found no place of peaceful rest,
Till Grace illumed my path, and now
  I lean upon my Saviour's breast.

Hope comes, commissioned from the skies,
  To dissipate my spirit's night,
But turns from earth her radiant eyes,
  And points to scenes of purer light.

The dearest joy this heart can know,
  The fondest bands that love can twine,
Lord, at thy feet I lay them low,
  Take all I have, and be Thou mine!

COMPOSED IN A GARDEN.

'Tis not the blossom-scented breeze,
  Nor rainbow dyes of flowers,
'Tis not the shade of vernal trees,
  Nor melody of bowers,
Though fragrant, soft, and fair they be,
That makes this scene so dear to me.

It is that *He*, the wondrous " Word,"
  That called them out of nought,
The presence of Creator's Lord
  Irradiates the spot.
There have I sought His face in prayer,
And He has deigned to meet me there.

There's not a little flower that springs
  Within this cultured bound,
Nor warbling bird, nor tree that flings
  Its graceful shadow round ;
But in its being I can prove
Some token of Jehovah's love.

The lily o'er her lowly bed,
   That bends her spotless form,
Tells me of Him who bowed His head
   Beneath wrath's dreadful storm ;
And when the Queen of Summer glows,
I think on "Sharon's matchless Rose."*

When clouds retire, and sunbeams bless,
   And Morn her freshness flings,
I see the "Sun of Righteousness
   With healing on His wings."
That glorious Sun ! whose potent ray
On darkness pours the living day !

I think, when 'neath some sheltering tree,
   I shun the noontide power,
So may my soul to Jesus flee
   In every trying hour ;
Beneath His shadow take her seat,
And taste His fruit and find it sweet.†

Or when th' aspiring cedar quakes
   Beneath the ruffling north,
Or gentle south each blossom wakes,
   And calls its spices forth ;
So with my soul The Spirit strives,
And every drooping grace revives.‡

* Canticles, ii. 1.   † Canticles, ii 3.   ‡ Canticles, iv 16.

I hear in every bird that sings
  The raptured notes of praise ;
Each insect opening its "glad wings "
  To sport in summer rays,
Unites with angels round The Throne,
To glorify the "Three in One."

"All thy works praise Thee," oh my God !
  And I that chorus love ;
But oh ! to quit this earthly load,
  And join the choir above,
There to behold Thee face to face,
And sing the triumphs of Thy grace.

When faith is swallowed up in sight,
  Then shall those joys be mine,
Then on " The Bride " with cloudless light,
  " The Bridegroom's " face shall shine.
No tears shall veil Him from Her eye,
And hope shall in fruition die.

STANZAS FOR SACRED MUSIC.

Wand'ring o'er this waste of sadness,
  What the weary pilgrim cheers?
What can raise his soul to gladness,
  Chase his doubts, and dry his tears?
'Tis the glance beyond to-morrow,
  'Tis the upward eye of faith,
Piercing through the cloud of sorrow,
  Smiles at danger, welcomes death.

Faith can joy in tribulation,
  Tracing still a Father's part,
Triumphs in the dear Relation,
  Clasps the promise to his heart,
Fears not though a host assail him,
  Safe in that unchanging love,
Which shall ne'er forsake nor fail him,
  Till he sit with Christ above.

COMPOSED IN THE PROSPECT OF AN UNEXPECTED RECOVERY FROM ILL-NESS.

Ah! where are the scenes so alluringly bright!
   The visions of glory that dawned on my view!
Alas! they are wrapped in the shadows of night,
   And I see them but distantly glimmering through.

My spirit exultingly thought how her chains
   At the voice of the Bridegroom would quickly be
      riven;
And I smiled on the fever that raged in my veins,
   For I hoped 'twas the chariot to bear me to Heaven.

No longer this earth had a share of my love,
   All its conflicts, its hopes, its enjoyments, were
      o'er:
I saw in Faith's vision my mansion above,
   Where sickness and sorrow should grieve me no
      more.

I saw the bright portals thrown open for me,
   And " Him that was slain " in the midst of " the
      Throne ;"
What sweetness ! what love in His face did I see,
   When He saw my white robe, and proclaimed it
      His own.

Methought the bright myriads that worshipped
   around,
   Gave glory to God for a sinner brought home,
While this song made the glorious Temple resound :
   " Come in, thou redeemed one ! for yet there is
      room !"

But ah ! while these scenes all my senses engage,
   And my soul, as a bird, soared to regions of day,
Health came like a foe to rebuild this dark cage,
   And she languishes still in her prison of clay.

Farewell ! ye sweet visions of glory and bliss,
   Methought a few hours would have made ye my
      own ;
And must I return to a desert like this ?
   Oh world! how insipid! how trifling thou'rt grown!

Must I still play my part on this mutable stage,
   And mingle once more with my brethren below ?
Must I still in the spiritual conflict engage,
   And groan 'neath the weight of my indwelling foe ?

Cease, murmurer, cease! thou proud rebel, be still;
   Presume not to question the Righteous Decree;
Oh, Father! conform my whole soul to Thy will;
   Then life, as Thy gift, shall be precious to me.

What though the crown glitters not yet on my brow,
   And the golden-stringed harp is withheld from
     my hand,
They are mine as securely as if I could now
   With Jesus my Saviour in Paradise stand.

Safe, safe in His keeping they're laid up for me,
   And I soon shall His power and faithfulness prove,
My own they are sealed by Eternal decree,
   And my Lord's is a fixed, an unchangeable love.

Thy glory, my God, is the end of my days,
   To Thy glory I'd live, to Thy glory I'd die;
May the time Thou'st assigned me be spent to Thy
     praise,
   Till Thou call me to join in Thy praises on high!

SUMMER EVENING BY THE SEA-SHORE.

A sunny beam yet lingers in the west,
  A trembling glory gilds the distant groves,
And Ocean, tranquil as a heart at rest,
  Breathes the low murmur meditation loves.

Eve's deep'ning shades are stealing o'er the wave,
  The moon is bright'ning in the deep blue sky ;
The busy, ruffling gale has ceased to rave,
  And the white sail glides swift and noiseless by.

In this delicious hour of calm repose
  The mourner's eye awhile may cease to weep ;
The wounded heart may slumber o'er its woes,
  Nor heave one sigh responsive to the deep.

Now soothed remembrance broods o'er vanished
      days,
  Reviews each form beloved, each blissful scene,
A word—a glance—with fond devotion weighs
  And lives regretted moments o'er again.

If the pale mourner on a scene like this
    Can gaze, with tearless eye, from anguish free ;
To peaceful bosoms, what an eve of bliss !
    Oh how extatic must such moments be !

For still as Memory sighs o'er parted hours,
    Hope lingers near—with liberal hand the while,
She strews th'untrodden path with fairer flowers,
    And lovelier prospects brighten in her smile.

TO C. C.

'Twas not the spirit of a love unblest,
  Chanting the funeral dirge of earthly pleasure—
'Twas not the anguish of a lonely breast
  Mourning the absence of its dearest treasure,
  That waked the trembling chords of that sad
    measure.

Not that the deep-toned plaints of settled woe
  Wrung from the tortured heart that hopes no
    healing,
But quiet tears, whose mild and tranquil flow,
  In brightness from the eye of sorrow stealing,
  Soothe and embalm the wounds of tender feeling.

Well hast thou deemed it was a withered flower
  That waked the thrilling sigh those notes are
    breathing;
I snatched a glowing rose from Friendship's bower,
  The fair deceit its thorny mischief sheathing.
  While on my heedless brow its buds were
    wreathing.

That rose of beauty in the past's dark tomb
　With many a kindred flower has long been
　　sleeping ;
But on the parent tree an embryo bloom
　Of future blossoms 'neath the leaves are peeping,
　Their infant charms with tears of Heaven weeping.

E'en like that rose, the moments that are fled,
　As fair their hue, as fragrant and as fleeting,
And forms as bright Hope's magic pencil spread
　As those sweet buds beneath their leaves re-
　　treating,
　While on their tender bloom the storm is beating.

Though the dishevelled rose lie pale in death,
　Though on her faded cheek no blush be glowing,
Yet in her bosom lives delicious breath,
　So from past joys a fragrance still is glowing,
　While memory all their early bloom is shewing.

THE FAREWELL.

Go—go, I feel 'tis best to part,
　Dear friend! how dear, I may not tell.
Alas! how can I teach my heart
　To bear that dreaded word, " Farewell!"

The blood must not forsake my cheek,
　No tear must in my eyelid swell,
No tell-tale sigh must dare to speak,
　How painful is the word " Farewell!"

When upon me, with parting gaze,
　Thy dark expressive eyes shall dwell,
How shall I meet their softened rays?
　How shall I see them look " Farewell!"

When some fair maid in distant land
　Pours on thy ear soft music's spell,
Remember her whose trembling hand
　Awaked for thee the strain " Farewell!"

When on the moon-illumined stream
　Thine eye with pensive gaze shall dwell,
Think how we watched her gentle beam—
　Oh! think upon our last " Farewell!"

IMPROMPTU,

TO S. T. ON HER BIRTH-DAY.

1822.

HAPLY, dear girl, thy ardent heart
  With many a wish is beating,
And Hope for thee a garland twines,
  Of flowers fair and fleeting.

Haply thou deem'st the fervent prayer,
  Breathed from true friendship's bosom,
Should be that thou may'st taste the fruit
  Of Hope's expanding blossom.

For thee I ask no earthly good,
  No sublunary pleasure,
Nor friendship true, nor faithful love,
  Nor health, that choicest treasure.

I will not wish thee length of days,
  Though warm the love I bear thee;
Thy friend, Susanna! has but one,
  One single wish to spare thee.

H

This, this, is still my earnest prayer,
　And oh! may grace receive it;
That He who bore the curse for thee,
　Would give thee to believe it.

Oh! what a gift were this, my friend!
　Beyond all thought it rises!
'Tis Christ himself! who in Himself
　All other gifts comprises.

If Christ be thine, Jehovah's thine,
　And nought His love can sever;
Then "present things, and things to come,"
　Are thine, and thine for ever!

SONNET.

How sweet ! to watch the Sun's slow lingering beam
  Stream o'er the west, and evening's bashful brow
  His farewell kiss receive, with roseate glow,
And timid flowers, that of late did seem
To shun with downcast eye his fervid gleam,
  Now lift their heads and blended fragrance throw,
  To bless the breeze that half forgets to blow ;
Reposing on their sweets, the sleeping stream
  No whispering leaf awakes. Oh moments bright !
When Contemplation heavenward lifts her eye,
  And tender Memory, with rapt delight,
Turns her full page, dear melancholy joy !
  Still be thou mine, when day's retiring light
Gleams faint and tremulous in the western sky.

TO THE ROBIN.

WARBLER of the rosy breast, and the merry spark-
　　ling eye,
Of all the birds I love thee best ; Robin, shall I tell
　　thee why ?
When the minstrel of the night from our groves
　　has taken flight,
When the merry Thrush is mute, hushed the Black-
　　bird's mellow flute,
When the seraph Lark no more his hymn of rap-
　　tured praise doth pour,
Then I hear thy cheerful lay, trilling through the
　　wintry day ;
Then I see, in many a row, thy tiny footprints in
　　the snow.
Duly as the morning comes, to seek thy dole of
　　scattered crumbs,
There thou art with head awry, and frequent hop
　　and glancing eye ;

Trusting Robin, come thou still to my well-spread
    window sill.

Well thou know'st there's nought to fear, thou art
    ever welcome here,

Warbler of the rosy breast! this is why I love
    thee best.

SHE MOURNETH IN SECRET.

This eye is never seen to weep,
　The world believes me gay ;
Within its chambers dark and deep,
My bosom's secret sorrows sleep,
　Hid from the garish day.

But oh when darkness wraps the skies,
　My restless couch I seek,
Night! thou art witness to my sighs,
My clasping hands, my streaming eyes,
　My pale, disordered cheek.

When peaceful bosoms find repose,
　I count each gloomy hour,
And if o'erspent with bitter woes,
My weary, aching eyelids close,
　Touched by the " balmy power."

Ah me! in visionary skies
　Unreal splendours gleam,
While phantom flowers gaily rise—
I start, I lift my languid eyes,
　And mourn the vanished dream.

IMPROMPTU.

In vain for me is nature robed in green,
  In vain for me each vernal bloom appears,
Ah me! how dimly are their beauties seen
  Through the sad medium of my falling tears.

Sweet Woodbine! wreathing o'er my fav'rite bower
  I twined thy garlands with a heart at rest ;
Sweet Rose! I trained thee from thy infant hour,
  And thought to wear thee on a peaceful breast.

'Tis not for me to pluck thy early bloom,
  'Tis not for thee to blossom o'er a heart
Whose hopes lie withering in the dark, cold tomb—
  Hopes, sweet and fair and fleeting as thou art.

A BOAT SONG.

SET TO MUSIC.

LIGHTLY o'er the azure tide
  Skims our fairy boat,
Gaily on the summer air
  Her silken pennons float.
Look! how the bright Sun
  Tints the golden west,
And curtains with purple
  His couch of rosy rest.

Robed in light, the Lily Queen
  Lifts her diadem,
Like Albion's fair and royal Dame,
  Begirt with many a gem;
The wavelets gather round her,
  And shield from danger nigh;
She's throned amid the waters,
  And heav'nward lifts her eye.

Sweetly on the heated brow
  Fans the twilight breeze,
Softly to his whispered vow
  Sigh the bending trees.
Now, while the moonlight
  Gems our sparkling way,
Rest we on our glancing oars,
  And chant our vesper lay.

Hark! hark! the dancing waves
  Have caught the choral strain,
And Echo from her mountain caves
  Reflects it back again.
Now let our light bark
  Wave her snowy wing,
And pour we forth our wild notes,
  Like joyous birds of spring.

TRANSLATED FROM THE FRENCH.

Oh! that I were a little bird!
  Beneath thy window every morn
  New melodies should wake the dawn;
I'd pour my raptured soul to thee,
And thou perhaps wouldst list to me,
                        Were I a little bird.

Oh! that I were a little bird!
  Thy steps I'd follow to the mead,
  Where thy pet lamb thou'rt wont to lead,
To browse upon the flowery grass,
And there the sultry noon I'd pass,
                        Were I a little bird.

Oh! that I were a little bird!
  At eve my tuneful breath I'd hold
  Within thy curtain's snowy fold;
Thence to thy fairy slipper creep,
And pass the night in blissful sleep,
                        Were I a little bird.

STANZAS SET TO MUSIC.

Stars of heaven! books of light!
Let me read your pages bright.
Say, does Laura gaze on ye?
Does she gaze, remembering me?
Could I read some message fair
Her bright eyes have written there?
Eyes whose sweetness o'er my soul
In light of dangerous beauty stole.
  Oh! what joy my heart would prove!
  Oh! how blest in Laura's love!

Rose of beauty, tell me why
Laura blushes when I sigh.
Is it scorn that fires her brow?
Is it Love's responsive glow?
Go, sweet rose, to Laura go,
On thy leaves I write my vow;
If a kiss on thee imprest
Bid thee welcome to her breast,
  Oh! what joy my heart would prove!
  Oh! how blest in Laura's love!

TO F——, WITH A KETTLE-HOLDER, ON THE 14th FEBRUARY.

When thy trim kettle sings its dreamy song,
  And thy lip quaffs the tea's refreshing balm,
May pleasing memories around thee throng,
  And o'er thy heart diffuse a soothing calm,
Clasp in thy hand this token of good will,
Which seeks from evil taint to guard it still;
Welcome it, Lady, though of homely frame,
Humble alike its office and its name.
True to its trust, 'twixt thee and harm it stands,
To guard from steam or stain thy gentle hands;
Apt emblem of thy friend, whose loving heart
Would gladly shield thee from affliction's dart.
Though taste and Nature's instincts may combine
To bid thee seek some other love than mine,
Yet shalt thou never find a *truer* Valentine.

STANZAS ADAPTED TO MUSIC.

On the merry, merry village bells!
How that peal my sad heart swells,
Calling from the tomb of years
Memories fraught with smiles and tears.
Oh the merry, merry village bells,
What a tale thy pealing tells!

Happy bride that beareth now
The white wreath on thy fairer brow,
May this peal in future days
Fill thy heart with grateful praise.
Oh, the merry, merry marriage bells,
How that sound thy young heart swells!

But should their altered tones awake
The knell that bids the fond heart ache;
Lift from earth thy tearful eyes,
Hark! the anthem of the skies!
A tale of loftier joy it tells,
More musical than marriage bells!

COMPOSED ON HEARING THE BELLS ON CHRISTMAS MORNING, 1859.

Welcome, auspicious day!
Day of the Saviour's birth;
Let the glad air the sound convey
Through the wide range of earth.

Lift up your voice, ye bells,
Ye sacred fanes resound,
Till the full pealing chorus swells
Triumphantly around.

Sing on, celestial train!
Circling the radiant Throne;
My heart responds the hallowed strain,
To mortal ear unknown.

And shall it be my own,
To join that white-robed Throng,
Cast at His feet my starry crown,
And harp th' untiring song?

Shall such a one as I,
  So weak, so frail, so base,
Wave the bright palm of victory,
  And wear the robe of grace?

Dwell with the blest above,
  From sin for ever free;
Shall I behold His looks of love,
  Who lived and died for me?

While hopes eternal and sublime
  Such healing balm impart,
No more the fleeting cares of time
  Shall desolate my heart.

Still as I tread the thorny way,
  No more by doubt opprest,
I'll look above the stars, and say,
  Yonder's my place of rest.

SOLEMN MUSINGS.

On Thou! who sitteth on that dreadful Throne,
Whose pillars are eternity; oh thou
Whose mighty arm upholds the universe!
Embracing all the varied forms of being,
From the archangel to the insensate clod;
Oh tell me, shall Thy creatures of the earth,
The dwellers of this mystic orb, e'er know
The secret springs, the complicated chains
That bind, propel, restrain this vast machine?
Shall they e'er grasp the mysteries of mind,
And reconcile, without a shadowy doubt,
Volition's freedom, with th' Eternal will!
Whence these high aspirations of the soul,
This quenchless thirst to know? are they of Thee?
Creator! Father! Author of all good!
I would not lift to the high throne of God
A bold, enquiring look; behold I bend
Low in the dust, and raise a suppliant eye,
Father! instruct thy child, nor let me lose

My wandering spirit, in the doubtful wilds,
Th' inextricable maze of human thought!
I look around upon this wondrous world,
Beautiful in its changes! whether fair Spring
Unfolds her laughing buds, or Summer glows
In plentitude of bloom, or Autumn wreathes
The vine's rich clusters in her yellow locks,
Or Winter stalks o'er the white mantled plain.
And sends his voice amid the trembling woods,
Oh Earth! how beautiful in all thy forms!
Whether thou lift thy mountain heights sublime,
Mocking the gorgeous clouds that float beneath,
Or sink into the fair luxuriant vale,
Or stretch in wild interminable wastes,
Or deep green woods, impervious to the day,
Or lighter groves, whose graceful shadows sport
With sunbeams glancing on the limpid brook
Thou wondrous world of waters! deep, sublime!
Circling with giant arms the beauteous earth,
What unseen force enchains thee in thy bed,
Thou raving maniac! leaping to the blast,
Hurling with desperate and remorseless power,
Like drifted weeds upon the fatal rock,
The floating castle with its living freight,
Tossing in scorn thy hoar and shaggy locks,
And shouting forth thy laugh of savage glee.

I

Sublimely dreadful in thy angry mood
Art thou, great Ocean! but thou hast thy phase
Of tranquil beauty, of voluptuous calm.
The passionate throbbings of thy mighty heart
Are stilled, and then thou liest in thy quiet bed,
Dimpling and smiling in thy blissful sleep,
Like a hushed infant on its mother's breast,
Breathing soft murmurs in its dreamy joy.
Then mirrored in thy crystal depths are seen
Things wondrous, quaint, and beautiful!
Myriad on myriads batten on thy stores,
And every floating weed and feathery spray
That clothe thy sparry grots are teeming all
With wondrous forms of strange, mysterious life.
And thou, ethereal Vast! whose azure vault
Bends with maternal care o'er earth and sea,
Thou bearest on thy brow that eye of flame
Which radiates heat, and light and life, and thence
Glides forth the Queenly Moon from her cloud
            canopy,
Gilding the ocean wave and flooding earth,
And sprinkling tree and tower with holy light.
And ye remoter worlds! ye countless stars,
Beautiful mysteries! say what are ye?
What is your mission? what your destiny?
Are ye the " Mansions of Our Father's House,"

Of which that blessed *Elder Brother* spake,
Who said, " I go your places to prepare ?"
There is such calm enchantment in your looks,
As to the gazer seems to promise rest,
When Earth, your fallen sister, shall arise,
Chastened and purified from penal fire,
When she hath yielded up her precious trust,
The buried seed of ages, to be clothed afresh
In robes of glory, fitted to receive
The spirit pure and holy, that, enshrined
In the Eternal bosom, still awaits
The promised blest reunion, shall not He
Who called ye forth, great host of rolling worlds,
People your orbs with blissful, endless life ?
Great God! it is enough for me to know
Thou art of life and love the bounteous source,
Thou hast no sympathy with pain and death,
Thy great creative power went forth to bless,
And Thou wilt perfect all thy grand design.

COMPOSED IN SICKNESS.

WELL, be it so—I'll not complain ;
And yet, to cheer the couch of pain,
Methinks I could awhile have borne
The rigour of a bleaker morn.

But oh, my soul! though many a plea
May keep my dearest friends from me,
Yet have I *One*, whose watchful love
Would never from my side remove.

He smooths the pillow for my head,
" Makes in my sickness all my bed ;"
His everlasting arms beneath
Would be my firm support in death.

My voice so feebly meets the ear,
Attention's self may fail to hear ;
But *One* my every want supplies
Before my faint petitions rise.

Weakness may need support awhile,
And even kindness dread the toil ;
But *One* untired, *One* faithful breast,
Would yield me an eternal rest.

My weak complainings tire and grieve
The friends who cannot all relieve ;
But *One* invites me to complain,
And sweetly soothes and heals my pain.

My kind Physician ! Brother—Friend !
On thee for healing I depend;
Thy precious balms can soothe my heart,
Though anguish tortures every part.

And while thy faithfulness I prove,
" Thy banner over me is love ;"
Not all the storms that o'er me roll,
Shall from her refuge shake my soul.

In sorrow's or temptation's hour,
While my frail nature owns its power,
The anchor of my soul shall be,
Firm " Rock of Ages," fixed on thee !

A BALLAD.

There was feasting and song in the baron's halls,
    And the lamps poured a flood of light,
And odorous flowers festooned the walls;
But the sweetest and loveliest blossom of all
    Was the baron's daughter that night.

There was many a dame of regal port,
    And maiden of beauty rare;
But Blanche appeared in such a sort,
As the Queen of beauty holding her court,
    And they but her handmaids fair.

Oh! many a fairy foot did bound
    To music's joyous tone;
Fair Sylph-like creatures floated round,
But neither form nor step was found
    So graceful as her own.

And many a voice awoke in song
    To the harp's inspiring swell,
Bearing the raptured sense along,
But Blanche, amid that warbling throng,
    Was the soul-stirring Philomel.

The noble, the wealthy, had sought her hand,
　And yeomen gallant and tall,
But little recked she of broad sword or broad land :
To her the red gold was but shining sand,
　And coldly she looked on them all.

Did scornful pride so rule her breast
　That she frowned alike on all ?
Ah no! one image her heart imprest,
Which threw its shadow on all the rest,
　And he was her father's Thrall !

Of goodly presence was he in truth,
　And lofty and noble his air ;
The Baron retained the stranger youth
As Ranger of park and woods, forsooth,
　Nor dreamed he of danger there.

" Raymond the Ranger" was all the name
　He e'er at the castle bore,
And whenever in quest of sylvan game,
In park or wood, the Ranger came,
　Blanche would be there before.

She comes to search for early flowers,
　And strawberries wild and sweet,
And thus she whiles the sultry hours,
Amid the warbling woodland bowers,
　A stag-hound at her feet.

And aye she pats the noble hound,
   While he with speaking eye
Licks the fair hand that gaily wound
A flowery chain his neck around,
   And bids the captive lie.

Ah, gentle Blanche! thy words are vain,
   When eager for the race,
With one glad bound he bursts the chain,
As Raymond stalks along the plain,
   Accoutred for the chase.

And still the Ranger lingers nigh,
   And bends with conscious grace,
While with slow step he passes by,
Well pleased to meet her downcast eye,
   And mark her blushing face.

One rosy eve Blanche sought her bower,
   Where cooed the turtle-dove,
And Philomel her soul did pour ;
Truly it was a witching hour
   For youthful hearts that love.

In secret Raymond watched hard by,
   And heard, 'mid musings sweet,
His murmured name, with gentle sigh,
And instant, with astonished eye,
   Blanche sees him at her feet.

With faltering tongue he then made known
    The secret of his heart,
And how to call her love his own,
He freely would renounce a throne,
    And from all glory part.

"Oh say that thou wilt be my bride,"
    He said with bended knee.
Then Blanche arose in stately pride:
"How canst thou dare, base churl," she cried,
    "Speak such wild words to me?

Rash youth! if to my noble Sire
    This insolence were known,
Thy life were forfeit to his ire,
By steel, by poison, or by fire;
    No mercy would be shewn."

Proudly he stood as Mountain Pine,
    Roused by this bitter scorn.
"Lady, my blood is pure as thine,
I sprang from e'en a loftier line
    Than that in which thou'rt born.

A cloud o'ershades my present life,
    The past is as a dream.
Thy pride is with thy love at strife,
No vassal asks thee for his wife,
    I am not what I seem."

Then to her wondering ear confest,
    Why he in base disguise
Unknown must for a season rest;
Then fervently his suit he pressed,
    With pleading voice and eyes.

She gazed upon his princely mien,
    His high and noble brow,
His steadfast eye assured and keen,
And sought her blushing face to screen,
    Love only triumphs now.

Her trembling hand she placed in his,
    Who clasped her to his heart,
And sealed the bond with love's first kiss.
Oh! in that sweet delirious bliss,
    How hard it is to part.

But hist! a rustling, crackling sound,
    As of some footstep near,
While Raymond fiercely glares around,
Blanche from his side with sudden bound
    Flies like a startled deer.

And thus upon the festal day
    They met, and sighed to part,
For she must lead the revels gay,
And he in solitude must stay,
    And school his jealous heart.

And pearls have wreathed her bosom fair,
    And clasped her arms of snow,
And gems are blazing in her hair,
But Blanche for these doth little care,
    He must not see her now.

'Mid the festive throng was a stranger guest,
    With a bearing of lofty degree ;
" I come, Lord Baron, as liketh thee best,
To join in thy revels and dance with the rest,
    Or measure broad swords with thee."

" Welcome, Sir Knight," the Baron replied,
    " Thy bearing is bold and free,
It were fitting to lay thy valour aside,
And choose from this circle of beauty's pride,
    The fairest thy partner to be."

" My noble host," said the Stranger Knight,
    " Thy garden of beauty is rare,
Its roses and tulips may dazzle my sight,
But the lily's robes are of woven light,
    And that is the flower I would wear."

The stranger glanced around the hall,
    Till the Lady Blanche he found,
He sought no more 'mid short or tall,
Hers was the form amongst them all
    That his vision of beauty crowned.

He takes her hand with trembling grasp,
    And her cheek wears the rose-bud's glow,
Ah! well she knows that tender clasp,
And the sweet breath came with panting gasp,
    And her cheek is pallid now.

The Baron marked her changing hue;
    " My child, what aileth thee ?
Nay, lead off without more ado,
Thy partner noble is, and true,
    Thou owest him courtesy."

Now Bruno, Raymond's favourite hound,
    Who tracked with mournful cries
His missing Master's footsteps round,
With tail erect and nose to ground,
    Straight to the castle hies.

He scratches at the half-closed door,
    Nor heeds the festal din,
The blazing lamps, the pictured floor,
The courtly figures gliding o'er,
    Fearless he rushes in.

He looked not right, he looked not left,
    But like an arrow fleet
Straight through the crowd his way he cleft,
And fawning on the stranger guest,
    Lay crouching at his feet.

The Baron's brow grew black as night,
　And wrathful flashed his eye.
" I know thee now, base stranger wight,
Unmask thee, churl! and no true knight,
　For this thou'rt doomed to die."

Forth rushed four stalwart serving men,
　To bind their master's Thrall.
Fierce as a lion in his den,
With savage growl roused Bruno then,
　And sprang upon them all.

" Down, Bruno, down!" the Ranger said,
　" What Fortune brought thee here?"
With courteous mien he bowed his head,
And paced the hall with stately tread,
　While all stepped back with fear.

For Bruno, still his jealous guard,
　Stalked grimly by his side,
With bristling coat and teeth all bared,
To keep each foe at bay prepared,
　Whatever might betide.

" Thy taunting words, my noble host,
　I pardon thee outright,
But know a lineage I boast
Noble as thine, and oft in joust
　Have proved myself true knight.

"In days of yore our house I ween
      Hath been to thine a foe;
For this I sought my name to screen,
For this have I a Ranger been,
      To win thy milk-white Doe.

" For her dear love I've served thee well,
      These twice twelve moons and o'er;
For her sweet sake content to dwell
Like Hart within my sylvan cell,
      And could for evermore.

" My sire now sleepeth his last sleep,
      Be thy feud buried there;
Of wrong, the brave no record keep,
When Death's cold hand in Lethe steep
      The grievances that were."

" Broad are my lands, my arm's renown
      Will not belie my race;
Grant me thy daughter for my own,
Freely I'd barter Scotland's crown,
      To win from thee this grace."

In bitter scorn the Baron cried,
      " Rather than child of mine
To thy accursed race allied,
Should grace thy halls and feed thy pride,
      Her death-doom I would sign.

" My only son thy father slew,
    And shall I end the strife ?
No—to my purposed vengeance true,
Thy father's heir shall have his due,
    I claim thy forfeit life."

" Now choose thee—on the gallows tree
    Thy airy dance to keep,
Or torn by blood-hounds would'st thou flee,
Or in the donjon pining be,
    Till thy last rotting sleep ?"

" Since my life's blood thy ire must slake,
    Baron, I'll sell it dear ;
I dare thy thralls my life to take ;
Thine own, for thy fair daughter's sake,
    From me hath nought to fear."

" Bold youth, thus far I'll do thee grace,
    And then our parley's done ;
Far as the bridge I grant thee space,
To keep unchecked thy stately pace,
    Then counsel thee to run."

Blanche clasps her hands in mute appeal,
    And seeks her father's eye ;
That eye was cold and hard as steel,
That vengeful heart no ruth could feel,
    Then came a piercing cry.

And lowly sinking on her knee,
      " Oh spare his life," she cried ;
" The stroke that sets his spirit free,
As surely will my passport be,
      Not death shall us divide."

" Hence to thy bower, I was to blame,
      I deemed thee pure and good ;
Thou art a scandal to my name.
Plead not for him, fond fool, for shame !
      Think on thy brother's blood !'

" In youthful heat thy noble son
      Provoked that luckless fight ;
'Twas in fair field the deed was done,
In knightly honour lost and won,
      The victory of that night."

Thus Raymond, as with footsteps free
      He gained the water's side ;
Up goes the creaking drawbridge high,
The Porter laughs with mocking eye,
      All egress is denied.

Ten archers range on the castle wall,
      With barb and bended bow ;
" Swim for thy life !" they loudly call.
" Swim ! Caitiff, swim, thy chance is small,"
      The Baron shouts below.

He plunges in the flashing wave,
  But another form is there;
An angel form is come to save;
She cries aloud, "True men and brave,
  Shoot boldly if you dare!"

That spectral form, like wreath of snow,
  On all has laid a spell;
The hound's unslipped, unbent each bow,
No danger threatens Raymond now,
  Sweet Blanche is loved too well.

She walks the waters by his side,
  But soon no footing found.
"Wind thy white arms round me," he cried,
"And mine shall buffet with the tide,
  And bring thee safe to ground."

Free on the waters all unbound,
  Bright streamed her sunny hair,
Her silken kirtle fluttered round,
And floated on, like a snow-white swan,
  The fearless maiden fair.

And they have swam the moat so wide,
  And safely gained the shore;
One moment are their forms descried.
With Bruno pacing by their side,
  And then are seen no more.

K

The Baron raved and tore his hair
    As he beheld his child
Thus for her love so boldly dare,
And each gay reveller rent the air
    With shrieks or accents wild.

Alas! for that unhappy sire,
    Blind fury rules his breast;
Parental love is lost in ire,
All night he feeds th' unholy fire,
    As if by fiends possest.

But morning comes, and with it grief
    That will not be supprest;
His looks are wan, his words are brief,
The wassail bowl brings no relief,
    The couch of down no rest.

Nor sylvan chase, nor hawk, nor hound,
    To him can pleasure give;
All former joys are tasteless found,
Since she to whom his heart was bound,
    For *him* has ceased to live.

But hatred to his ancient foe
    Hath dried affection's spring,
And though he pines in lonely woe,
Yet he disdains to seek *her* now,
    Who left his sheltering wing.

And now Fitzallan, free as air,
 Abandons all disguise,
Soothing her grief with gentle care,
Straight to a holy father bare
 His fair and fainting prize.

The wondering Priest their story hears,
 Their dripping garments dried,
With holy words dispelled her fears,
And ere the morning sun appears,
 Blanche is Fitzallan's bride.

A Prince is he in his domain,
 With nobles at his call ;
And Blanche in royal guise doth reign,
Surrounded by a courtly train,
 The fairest of them all.

And she is blessed in her liege lord,
 And blest in her is he;
All the delights of life outpoured
Upon the loving pair are showered,
 Who bounteous are and free.

Thus was their wedded life begun,
 And then, to crown the rest,
Before twelve moons their course had run,
Fitzallan sees his infant son
 Clasped to his mother's breast.

And Blanche assumes the pleasing care
    That tender mothers shew,
And bending o'er her blossom fair,
She weeps to think Fitzallan's heir
    May ne'er his grandsire know.

She knoweth now the yearning love
    Which throbs a parent's heart,
That steady fire all flames above
Nor guilt can quench, nor absence move,
    To smoulder or depart.

Pallid and wan grows Blanche's cheek,
    And sunk her heavy eye;
Her step is slow, her nerves are weak,
She feels a grief she dares not speak,
    Save in a faltering sigh.

She pines for him, the lonely one,
    Her childless greyhaired sire;
She broods o'er days for ever gone,
When his fond eye indulgent shone
    On all her young desire.

She longs to bathe his hand with tears,
    And clasp his honoured knee;
To win acceptance for her lord,
To hear him speak the pardoning word,
    And bless their progeny.

Fitzallan marked her altered tone:
   " Sweet love, declare to me
What is thy wish? it shall be done:
Is there a good beneath the sun,
   I would deny to thee?"

" Oh! bear me to my father's seat,
   To seek his dear loved face,
To bathe with duteous tears his feet,
A blessing for our child entreat,
   For *us* forgiving grace!

So will my cheek renew its bloom,
   My heart be light and free;
His daughter to an early tomb
A father's curse would surely doom,
   It presseth heavily."

Six prancing steeds were harnessed straight,
   Swift on their way they went;
Fitzallan and his lady wait
A parley at the castle gate,
   And forth a white flag sent.

Before the year its course had run,
   The Baron's anger past,
He yearns to clasp his only one,
To own Fitzallan for his son,
   And heal the feud at last.

A messenger he sends before,
    Bearing the flag of peace ;
And words of pardoning grace he bore,
With welcome to a father's door,
    And love no more to cease.

Upon the bridge the white flags meet,
    And glad shouts rend the air,
The Baron comes his guests to greet,
Fold to his heart his daughter sweet,
    And bless Fitzallan's heir !

TO ———.

We have met, my friend, and the lapse of years,
And the sorrows that open the fount of tears,
   Have sprinkled our locks with grey;
But our hearts are yet green in their fadeless truth,
And the kindly feelings which blessed our youth,
   Not yet have passed away.

Thou art sad, my friend, and thy drooping gaze
Too painfully telleth of cheerless days,
   And the lonely spirit's blight;
Our path in life hath been wide apart,
But we each know the throb of a sensitive heart,
   And feeling which shrinks from the light.

Springs there no flower in thy desolate way?
Warbles no bird its Heaven-taught lay,
   To cheer thy lonely hearth?
Then turn thee to Him, whose bleeding brows
Wore a chaplet of thorns for thy soul's repose,
   He can make thee a Heaven on earth.

Then cheer thee, dear friend of my early youth,
Drink deep from the fount of eternal truth,
   Thy faltering steps to aid.
Oh ! lift thine eye to the realms above,
And seek in those regions of light and love
   For the flowers that never shall fade.

JUVENILE POEMS;

PRINCIPALLY WRITTEN BETWEEN THE AGE OF
TEN AND SIXTEEN YEARS.

ON THE DEATH OF MY BELOVED MOTHER.

COMPOSED IN MY TENTH YEAR.

In yon churchyard lies my best friend,
   Too worthy in this world to stay;
'Twas God's own will her life should end,
   So bore her sainted soul away.

And now above she happy soars,
   Perhaps looks down with pitying eye,
To see how many still deplore
   The hapless day that saw her die.

Alas! the partner of her life,
   Long must he pine in lonely grief,
Still must he mourn his dear lost wife,
   Till in the grave he find relief.

And ah ! her children left behind
    For ever must her loss deplore,
Till that far happier home they find,
    And meet with her to part no more.

Our wise Creator deemed amiss
    That one so good on earth should be ;
Now her reward is heavenly bliss,
    I'll strive to prove as good as she.

Then my abode shall be on high,
    No earthly cares shall there be found ;
And while I dwell above the sky,
    I'll pitying look on earthly ground.

FAREWELL TO A FAVOURITE NURSE.

ELIZABETH, must you be gone,
And must I say adieu?
Must I your loss for ever moan?
Alas! it is too true!

So greatly I the past regret,
The tears stream from my eye,
I almost wish we ne'er had met,
These eyes had then been dry.

But yet amid this parting pain,
One thought my bosom cheers,
We only part to meet again,
Then I'll dry up these tears.

My baby sister, dearest nurse,
You may entrust to me;
I'll be a mother to that babe,
Though but a child I be.

When thou art gone, her wondering eyes
    Will seek for thee in vain;
Rocked in my arms, I'll hush her cries,
    And make her smile again.

Oh think of me when far away,
    And I will think on thee,
And night and morning will I pray
    That thou mayst happy be.

The hour is come, oh, bitter woe!
    When thou and I must part.
Farewell! then since it must be so,
I dare not wait to see thee go,
    That sight would break my heart!

ALWYN AND EVELINA.

A FACT VERSIFIED IN MY ELEVENTH YEAR.

Alas! who is that melancholy maid?
  Her lily hands crossed on her woe fraught breast;
Tell me for whom she heaves the bursting sigh,
  Oh, say the cause that robs her heart of rest.

'Tis Evelina, charming, hapless maid,
  The youthful prey of overwhelming grief;
O'er Alwyn's urn she droops, whom cruel death
  Untimely snatched, and robbed her of relief.

The morn was sparkling, smiling, and serene,
  The village bells pealed forth a sound divine;
A lovely youthful pair as e'er were seen
  Their vows to plight, now bowed at Hymen's
    shrine.

Content and pleasure sparkled in each eye,
   Good wishes followed them from every side,
And all the village echoed to the cry,
   " Long live young Alwyn and his lovely bride !"

The bridal ceremony o'er,
   With joyful hearts they trip away ;
A press-gang soon impedes their course,
   And fix on Alwyn for their prey.

In vain she wept, in vain she prayed,
   Nor tears nor prayers the wretches move ;
Now at their feet she wildly kneels,
   " Oh, kill me ! but release my love."

The Press-gang tore him from her sight,
   Her to their home kind neighbours bore ;
" My love ! my life ! my Alwyn's gone,
   And I shall see his face no more !"

Twelve months in lonely grief she passed,
   No tidings met her anxious ear;
The battle o'er, peace came at last,
   The bells proclaimed the victors near.

And now, enraptured at the news,
   On wings of love away she flew,
To meet her soldier in the grove,
   Whose altered face she scarcely knew.

His cheek, once blooming as the rose,
   A deadly pallor now o'erspread,
And the bright locks that graced his brows,
   Were thinly scattered o'er his head.

"Ah, cruel, cruel war!" she cried,
   "That cost my Alwyn so much woe!
A tender nurse thou'lt find thy bride,
   And we shall both be happy now."

"Alas! my love!" he faintly said,
   "My wounds are dangerous and deep—
I can no more—oh, cruel death!"
   Then sank a corpse close at her feet.

Oh, stranger! think what bitter grief,
   Forced from her love again to part.
She shed no tear o'er Alwyn's grave,
   But silent woe consumes her heart.

THE FLOWER GARDEN.

WITHIN my garden's calm retreat,
  Where various flowers bloomed around,
I strolled, and as I viewed each sweet,
  Believed myself on Fairy ground.

Beneath a Lilac's tempting shade,
  The Lily-of-the-vale was seen;
Who modest, veiled her spotless head
  Within her folds of lively green.

And near the spot, well-nigh concealed,
  The lowly Violet did spring;
But Zephyr oft the flower revealed,
  And bore her fragrance on his wing.

The Hyacinth, whose azure bells
  Hung pendant from her spiry stalk,
And Mignonette diffused their spells,
  And with sweet odours filled the walk.

And there, within her leafy bed,
    The rural Primrose shewed her face ;
And Cowslips, natives of the mead,
    In sweet profusion decked the place

High up the wall the Jasmine climbed,
    And mid her stars of snowy hue,
The blushing Eglantine entwined,
    Still sparkling with the early dew.

In simple vest the Woodbine clad,
    Fondly embraced her neighbouring flower ;
And mingling sweets their beauties spread,
    And shed their aromatic power.

Laburnum, with wide spreading boughs,
    Her wreaths of gold above them hung ;
And many a friendly shrub arose,
    To shield them from the noonday sun.

But oh ! the sweetest and the best,
    And loveliest flower of all that blows,
A Rosebud peeping mid the rest,
    Began its beauties to disclose.

And while I yet admiring stood,
    To watch her form maturer grow,
The blushing floaret, as I viewed,
    With deeper blushes seemed to glow.

                                L.

Next morn I rose and sought the spot
　　Which lately gave so much delight;
Ah! as I went, I little thought
　　To view the ravages of night.

Nought of my favourite could I see,
　　Till looking earnestly around,
I viewed the poor forsaken tree,
　　And Rose-leaves scattered on the ground.

'Tis thus, alas! with joys we prize,
　　Thus life's fair flowers are blooming gay;
But when misfortune's storms arise,
　　The withered blossoms strew the way.

TO A ROBIN WHICH DROPPED ON THE FLOOR IN A HALF FROZEN STATE.

Poor little Bird, thou com'st in woful plight,
  Thy trembling limbs are numbed by the chill
      wind;
Here sleep securely through the wintry night,
  Warm as my hearth the welcome thou wilt find.

Come, trembler, come, and warm thee in my breast,
  Needless thy doubt, and vain thy timid fear;
Oh let that fluttering heart subside to rest,
  Welcome, my little favourite, welcome here!

Be my companion while the drifting snow
  Mantles the scene; for ah! thy natal trees
Afford no food nor shelter for thee now,
  With hunger thou must pine, with cold must
      freeze.

'Twould please me much to see thee sit and preen
  Thy rosy breast and plume thy glossy wing;
Or perched upon my chair or loftier screen,
  Thine own wild notes melodiously sing.

I'll shelter thee from cold and every wrong,
  I'll spread thy little banquet day by day;
When spring returns repay me with thy song,
  And thou shalt freely hop from spray to spray.

No latticed cage my Robin shall confine,
  Free shall he be to take his early flight;
Breathe the fresh air upon the lofty pine,
  Or taste the ripened berry's sweet delight.

Mine is no tyrant's hand to bid thee mope
  Within thy wiry prison's narrow bound,
To watch thy feathered mates in freedom group,
  Rocked on the trees or fly their airy round.

When the glad earth throws off her snowy screen
  And budding trees proclaim the coming spring;
Then, little Pensioner, shalt thou be seen,
  Hopping the turf and stretching thy free wing.

ON SEEING CHILDREN BUILDING HOUSES WITH CARDS.

WHEN builds some Innocent, in earnest play,
  The paper edifice with careful hands;
If chance an urchin, mischievously gay,
  Shake the unsteady plain on which it stands,

Down in an instant falls each painted room,
  Each gilded column strews the faithless plain;
Awhile the Infant mourns its ruined dome,
  Then with new ardour falls to work again,

And thus it is in solitary hours
  Creative Fancy rears a structure gay;
She wreaths the pile with amaranthine flowers,
  And flings each thorn and noisome weed away,

But should a step the solitude invade,
  Or foliage tremble in a ruder blast,
The structure falls, the beauteous chaplets fade,
  And all the visionary bliss is past.

Oh, strange vicissitudes of joy and grief!
  For should that footstep die upon the ear,
Or should the breeze be hushed that waved the
      leaf,
  Again the fair aërial forms appear.

Oh, Fancy! still at meditative Eve
  Renew thy work, so exquisitely fine;
Dull probability to others leave,
  Be thy enraptured visions ever mine.

ON A HEARTSEASE THAT BLOOMED THROUGH THE YEAR.

THERE is a little, laughing flower,
  That fearless looks on Winter's face,
And vainly strives the tyrant power
  To rob her of one simple grace.

I marked her when the Autumn Rose
  Its lingering blossoms palely spread;
I marked her when December's snows
  Fell lightly o'er her frozen bed.

I marked her when the ruthless gale
  Tore the dark branch from many a tree;
I marked her 'mid the pelting hail,
  The patient flower still smiled on me,

As if she saw the future day,
  When wintry storms shall sink to rest,
When light-winged zephyrs softly play
  O'er blossomed sweets on Maia's breast.

Now virgin Snowdrops newly blown,
　　Bend toward earth the timid eye,
As if they feared the parting frown
　　Of their stern sire yet lingering by.

Ere Winter from the scene withdrew,
　　His icy fingers formed the flower,
Spring streaked it with her emerald hue,
　　And smiled and triumphed in her power.

In gorgeous robes the Crocus drest,
　　Now closes 'mid the changeful day,
Now pleased expands her radiant vest,
　　To catch the Sun's congenial ray.

In softest purple tints arrayed,
　　Close at their feet the Violet springs,
And 'mid her leaves' luxuriant shade
　　Her perfume on the breeze she flings.

The Hawthorn falls in slender wreaths,
　　Gemmed with fair Nature's darling hue;
The Primrose meekly lurks beneath,
　　And bathes her paly cheek in dew.

And near that flower so meek and pale,
　　Fond Zephyr oft suspends his wing,
The Cowslip's honied breath to steal,
　　And breathe abroad the varied spring.

But these, when Summer heats advance,
  And Roses blush with infant day,
These, sinking from the fervid glance,
  Shall sigh their fragrant souls away ;

While thou, unchanged, unfading flower,
  When all their timid beauties cease,
Shall still adorn my favoured bower,
  And cheer it with thy smile of peace.

Thus, while I mourn departed days,
  (Pale, faded flowers in fancy's eye,)
Thus Hope with smiling patience stays,
  And points to scenes of future joy.

TO M. M., WITH VIOLETS.

Ere the young buds revealed their purple hue,
    I marked, dear friend, these violets for thee;
Early each morn I hastened where they grew,
    And watched with tender care their infancy.

But when bright Sol, to renovate the day,
    Appeared with splendour in the blue serene
They gave their fragrance to his cheering ray,
    And burst at length their covering of green.

With joy each spring I hail this darling flower,
    Its modest merit yields a charm for me,
But doubly now I own its pleasing power,
    Since, Margaretta, it is prized by thee.

TO LAURA.

AN INVOCATION TO RISE.

Now Morning, with refulgent eye,
    Looks up from Ocean's crystal caves,
And bids the rose-tinged vapours fly,
    And gilds the curtain of the waves.

Laura, thy laughing eyes unclose,
    Rise ere the bright hues speed away ;
Ah ! would'st thou give to dull repose
    The first, best moments of the day ?

R'se, that the balmy breath of morn
    May give her freshness to thy brow ;
Lift thy light ringlets, and adorn
    Thy cheek with youth's extatic glow.

Though Ocean smiles so blue, so fair,
    Not yet we'll rove his pebbly shore,
For chilling gales still linger there,
    And toss the foam-crowned billow o'er.

But when the winds no longer rave,
    Again we'll seek the murmuring strand,
Cull the bright treasures of the wave,
    That gleam upon the golden sand;

Or mark the sea-fowl's circling wing,
    And see her stem with snowy breast
The azure tide, and wild notes sing,
    To charm the list'ning waves to rest.

While yet the Spring is dim and pale,
    We'll stray amid our cultured bowers,
Mark the first Snowdrop's graceful bell,
    And bless the pledge of brighter hours.

Still as we view that flowret fair,
    Fancy's keen eye shall pierce the gloom,
Hang with fresh green the branches bare,
    And deck the scene with Summer's bloom.

ON THE DESERTED COTTAGE ON DUN-WICK CLIFF.

On the cliff's rugged brow, that o'erlooks the wide
    ocean,
  All wild and deserted a lone cottage stood;
Rounds its desolate walls the long grass was in
    motion,
  The lizard's and toad's unmolested abode.

Ah, sadly it stood like the hall of desertion,
  Within all was silent, without all was still;
Save the billows' low music, that seemed in diver-
    sion
  Each other to chase to the steep chalky hill.

The light osier fence which the garden surrounded
  In withered disorder lay quite overthrown.
Encumbering the borders it lately had bounded,
  And the paths with rank nettles and weeds were
    o'ergrown.

One poor little flower to the desert soil clinging,
    Just marked out the spot where its sisters had
        been ;
On the breeze its pale blossoms so carelessly
      swinging,
    As heedless of beauty that seldom was seen.

As a maiden bereft of her kindred and lover,
    Still haunts the sad spot which received their
      cold earth,
Still loves in pale grief o'er their ashes to hover.
    So watched that lone flower o'er the place of its
      birth.

TO SPRING.

On, fairest of the year! delightful Spring!
   How oft thy name has waked the poet's song,
How shall I dare attempt the joys to sing,
   And countless graces that to thee belong!

Yet when I view the eye-refreshing green
   That clothes the branches of yon graceful trees,
And the fair blossom gaily peep between;
   Ah, how can I forbear mid scenes like these?

Alas! I've little power thy praise to speak,
   Unskilled to touch the Lyre with magic art;
Yet the warm tear that trembles on my cheek,
   Is the pure language of a grateful heart.

Ye that can rove with cold, unsearching eye,
   Whose frigid souls fair Nature ne'er could melt,
Who pass her beauties all unheeded by;
   Will laugh at raptures which ye never felt.

But ye whose hearts a ray of feeling warms,
　　Come rove with me o'er yon delightful plain,
Where every hedgerow boasts a thousand charms,
　　And every field is rich in waving grain.

The desert heath erewhile so drear and sad,
　　With golden blossoms is profusely gay;
The slender Harebell in soft azure clad,
　　And Hyacinths their purple charms display.

There on the yielding turf, with moss o'ergrown,
　　The little Heathbell blooms with simple grace;
And Nature with a lavish hand hath thrown
　　Unnumbered sweets to decorate the place.

Far o'er the hedge with many a curling wreath,
　　In wild luxuriance, the Woodbine grows;
The little Violet seeks the shade beneath,
　　And fragrant Brier unfolds its blushing Rose.

The Hawthorn sparkling in the dews of morn,
　　The drooping Cowslip and the primrose pale,
In sweet disorder all the banks adorn,
　　And charge with balmy breath the playful gale.

While o'er these scenes my eye delighted strays,
　　Oh! let me not forget by whom they're given.
So every charm that draws the curious gaze,
　　May lift my soul in gratitude to Heaven.

TO MARY.

Oh! Mary, when this humble shed
   Shall hear thy gentle voice no more,
When thy light step shall cease to tread
   This garden's little boundary o'er—

Oh! sometimes let thy fancy rove
   From happier scenes to this lone spot ;
Oh, spare one little beam of love,
   To brighten this forsaken cot.

Oh, spare one little tender thought,
   To hover o'er these drooping bowers,
Deserted by the hand that taught
   Their shade to bless the sultry hours.

When thou art gone, thy sister's hand
   Shall foster well thy favourite tree,
And while beneath its shade I stand,
   I'll breathe a fervent prayer for thee.

M

ELEGY ON A PET LEVERET.

Soon as thy timid eye beheld the light,
  Poor little orphan, mis'ry marked thy way ;
Thy tender mother, hurried from thy sight,
  To savage greyhounds fell a hapless prey.

Then by the fond maternal care unblessed,
  Soon had thy little form resigned its breath,
But soft compassion touched the sportsman's breast,
  He stretched his hand, and rescued thee from
    death.

'Twas mine to shield thee from the chilling air,
  'Twas mine to act the nurse's tender part ;
I fed, I watched thee with the fondest care,
  And hushed the throbbings of thy fearful heart.

Ah, what availed the generous wish to save,
  The warm asylum and the fragrant bed ;
Thy beating heart lies quiet in the grave,
  Where pitying flowers bend o'er thy lifeless
    head.

No Willow shades thy couch of lowly sleep,
  No Cypress spreads its dark funereal gloom,
But the sweet Rose with tears of Heaven doth
      weep,
  And scatter o'er thy turf her earliest bloom.

164

A SATIRE IN IMITATION OF HORACE.

IMPROMPTU.

LESBIA, the little and the vain,
Anxious a lover to obtain,
  Employs each female art;
Bedecked with silks, and flowers, and lace,
She flits about from place to place,
  And tries each dandy's heart.

Each fancied grace the nymph unfurls,
With studied ease her countless curls
  In bright redundance flow;
Vain as that fly, of rainbow wing,
That revels with the flowers of spring,
  She flutters round each Beau.

She sees some active youth advance,
And instant, in the mazy dance
  Her utmost skill she tries;
With languid swim, or airy bound,
She seeks amid the festive round
  To lure some coxcomb's eyes.

But Lesbia plays a different part,
When doomed to practise on the heart
   Of Bachelor staid and prim ;
She praises all his prudent ways,
Her culinary art displays,
   And flatters every whim.

Maid of the soft and flexile mind,
How kindly, still thou art inclined
   To cherish Sage or Beau ;
Ah cruel ! should the Fates ordain
That little Lesbia should remain
   In cheerless single woe.

Forbear, fond maid, these fruitless arts,
Confine thy powers to making tarts,
   Or garnishing a dish ;
Scorn the vile sex ! and take instead,
A little Beau of gingerbread,
   And mould him to thy wish.

TO A FRIEND WITH THE FIRST VIOLET.

When Tyrant Winter quits the plain,
And Spring resumes her gentle reign,
I search each bank and hedgerow wild
For thee, sweet flower, her darling child.
The balmy breath of western breeze,
That waved the flowers and kissed the trees,
Revealed thee in thy shy retreat,
And wafted me thy odours sweet.
I saw thee bow thy modest head,
To hide within thy leafy bed,
And snatched thee from that sylvan bower,
Sweet Violet! purple-vested flower.
Awhile upon my breast recline,
Awhile thy fragrance shall be mine ;
  Then, little favourite, must thou hie,
Far from the scenes that gave thee birth,
  To soothe *her* heart, and please *her* eye,
Who loves thy unassuming worth ;

And when thou shalt her breast adorn,
Say how I went at early morn,
And tended thee with careful hand,
And watched thy infant charms expand.
And when, oppressed by solar rays,
Thou languished in the noontide blaze,
How oft the kind relief I'd bring,
Of liquid crystal from the spring.
Tell her, though soon thy bloom must fade,
Thy dying odour must be shed ;
Yet, if 'tis mine again to view
Fair Spring resume her vernal hue,
I'll search the spot where first my eye
Glanced on thy wild simplicity,
And rove the infant shades among,
To find thy fairest sister throng.
And sure *their* lot and *thine* were blest,
To wither on so true a breast.

"THE WIND PASSETH OVER IT, AND IT IS GONE."

The Lark poured forth her melody,
  Oh! 'twas a morning fair,
The dew-steeped grass was scarcely dry,
Serenely smiled the azure sky,
  No vapour floated there;
But soon black clouds came rolling by,
  And thunder rent the air.

The Ocean as it softly crept,
  A soothing murmur gave,
So calm, so smooth, so still it slept,
The Zephyr that its bosom swept,
  Scarce curled the silver wave;
Not long this peace the ocean kept,
  I saw it foam and rave.
Where many a Sister flower grew,
  A lovely Rose I found.
Still sparkling with the early dew,
And far the blushing beauty threw

Her fragrant breath around;
A gust of lingering winter blew,
  And dashed her to the ground.

Oh, may it teach my heart to prize
  Life's pleasures as they are,
To fix my hopes beyond the skies;
Whatever griefs may then arise,
  Whatever ills I bear,
I'll Heav'nward turn my wishful eyes,
  And find my solace there.

TO MARY WITH A BASKET OF FLOWERS.

RECEIVE this basket, dearest Maid,
　With every Floral beauty crowned
That scents my bower's delicious shade,
　Or blooms within the garden's bound.

Fresh from soft April's gilded showers,
　The Violet see in vernal pride ;
And Jonquils bright with golden flowers,
　Bend by the fair Narcissus' side.

These, rich in ruby's deepest hue,
　Auricula with lavish bloom ;
There Hyacinths white and azure blue,
　Mingle their tints and rich perfume.

And there the flower of varied dye,
　Close by the Primrose pale and meek :
And there, in regal majesty,
　Anemone with glowing cheek.

Conspicuous in her brilliant dress,
  The Heartsease lights up every flower;
Oh! may her presence ever bless
  My Mary's path, my Mary's bower.

IMPROMPTU.

Though Fate denied my humble prayer,
To breathe the evening's perfumed air,
Yet in your joys I have a share—My Sisters!

This purple Thyme, and Violet sweet,
Culled from the hedgerow's green retreat,
With added charms my senses greet—My Sisters!

This Hawthorn, with its blossomed snow,
Has brought my heart a warmer glow
Than if these eyes had seen it grow—My Sisters!

The simple gift so kindly made,
To memory's cell shall be conveyed,
And there its hues shall never fade—My Sisters!

LINES.

I THOUGHT as I wandered from home,
  I had left every comfort behind;
And I wept at the merciless doom
  That tore me from beings so kind.

The moments passed languidly by,
  And I longed for the hour of repose,
For then unobserved I might sigh,
  And brood o'er my heart's secret woes.

I could think on the days that are gone,
  The days I can never forget;
I could linger o'er joys I have known,
  Nor check the fond tear of regret.

Thou pillow canst witness my grief,
  When my cheek thy kind refuge hath prest,
Did its softness e'er give me relief?
  Did its smoothness compose me to rest?

SUPPOSED TO BE WRITTEN BY A DIS-APPOINTED LOVER.

WHERE are the tranquil joys I late possest?
  Why does the ready tear unbidden start?
Why from my pillow flies its balmy rest?
  And why art thou so sad, my fluttering heart?

Sportive as Zephyr on a summer morn,
  My heedless footsteps sought a fairy bower,
I saw a Rose, and, reckless of the thorn,
  I bent to gaze on the fair, treacherous flower.

Sure 'twas the sweetest bud that e'er revealed
  Its bashful beauty to th' admiring gaze;
But ah! those charms the lurking foe concealed,
  That dim the prospect of my future days.

While yet my youthful heart throbbed high with
      hope,
  And Fancy wove her wild, romantic scheme,
Pale Disappointment came, and rudely shook
  The baseless fabric of my airy dream.

Wide o'er the scene she stretched her dusky wing,
   And breathed a poison on the coming hours,
Like those bleak, chilling blasts in early spring
   That blight the fairest of her infant flowers.

As the last beam that gilds the fading sky,
   When Phœbus hastens to his western goal,
So Hope's last ray still trembles in my eye,
   And sheds a lingering brightness on my soul.

LOVE'S LOGIC.

Oh tell, tell me not of Love,
  My heart disowns the wayward power :
Through life's fair scenes I mean to rove.
  Untempted by that treacherous flower.

How oft the fair wild Rose we meet,
  All sparkling with the dews of morn ;
Looking so innocently sweet,
  But ah ! beware the lurking thorn.

Nay, talk no more of Love to me,
  It is at best a feverish dream ;
Full swiftly would the vision flee.
  Chased by the morn of Reason's beam.

Love as a foaming torrent seems
  Impetuous, rushing o'er a steep,
But Friendship is a gentle stream,
  In whose calm wave the moonbeams sleep.

But what, Alexis, dost thou say,
   That Love with Friendship is combined?
And though with Youth Love speeds away,
   Yet Friendship still is left behind?

Ah! plainly then indeed appears,
   To slight your counsel would be wrong,
Since Love can gild our early years,
   And Friendship last our whole lives long.

LITTLE ALICE.

A RIDDLE.

LITTLE Alice is gone to her early rest,
　　And a tear is in her eye,
For the Sun has flung from the golden west
The crimson folds of his gorgeous vest,
　　And they float in the deep blue sky,
And the child had gazed till it throbbed her breast
　　With emotions new and high.

Little Alice has pillowed her glowing cheek,
　　And she cannot choose but weep;
For her upturned eyes so blue and meek,'
Are watching the change of each fiery streak
　　That between the curtains peep,
Till the sweet lids drooped like a closing flower,
　　And she sunk in a tranquil sleep.

Through her parted lips, as a rose-bud fair,
　　Bedropped with pearly dew,
The sweet breath passed like a spicy air,
And stirred the ringlets of golden hair

That over her temples flew ;
While the sultry breath of the summer air
  Heightened her roseate hue.

Sleep on, fair child, for the time draws near
  When thou shalt sleep no more.
Already a voice assails thine ear,
Which is ever to thee a sound of fear,
  In the dreary midnight hour.
Awake! awake! thy foe is near,
He hath wound his horn, he hath couched his spear.
  It is dripping with crimson gore !

He came like a pilgrim robed in grey,
  Hymning a vesper song ;
He stole to the couch where the young child lay
Like a dew-spangled Rose or a sleeping Fay,
  And he mustered his blood-thirsty throng,
While the holy strain changed to a Roundelay,
  Fearfully shrill and strong.

Right valiantly grappled the little maid
  With her fierce and wily foe,
She uttered no cry, she sought no aid,
While that furious troop the onslaught made ;
  But she dealt them many a blow,
Till many a glittering spear was stayed,
  And plumed helm laid low.

Thus Alice spent the long, long night,
   And she joyfully hailed the day,
When the Sun looked forth in a flood of light,
And put her terrible foes to flight,
   Who stealthily sneaked away.
But they vowed at eve to renew the fight,
And furbished their blood-stained weapons bright,
   Whilst they in ambush lay.

   Reader, unfold the flimsy veil
   Which seeks to mystify my tale,
   And say who were the midnight foes
   That broke the little maid's repose ?

ORIGINAL ENIGMAS, CHARADES, ETC.

ENIGMA I.

Ah! once I revelled wild and free,
O'er battle-field or flowery lea ;
My graceful form no fetters bound,
I danced in air or swept the ground.
My sire, though somewhat old and grey,
Had been a trooper in his day,
And then it was a great delight
To train his offspring for the fight.
Teach me to parry thrusts and blows,
And scatter our blood-thirsty foes.
When he to sylvan sports inclined,
I always followed close behind,
Or if he figured in the race,
I ever kept an equal pace :
Thus unrestrained my youth I passed,
But "life's young dream" is fled at last!

While I was sporting in my pride,
Some wretch my fine proportions spied,
Me by my locks the felon took,
And my whole form he rudely shook;
Stretched on the rack my helpless frame,
My stubborn will to bend and tame;
From all this suffering is it strange
That o'er me came a wondrous change?
My form once flexile, now is tough,
Bony and sinewy enough;
Once slender, now where'er I stand,
I cover some extent of land;
Since from my parent I was torn,
I am so altered and so worn,
That those who formerly knew me,
Would doubt of my identity;
Besides my pristine name I've lost,
And bear another to my cost,
For wheresoever it is heard,
'Tis smiled at as a thing absurd.
I crowd the court, the park, the ring,
In fashion's haunts I take my swing,
Yet though grave folks affect to flout me,
Yet very few will do without me.

ENIGMA II.

Look through your wardrobe, lady—am I there?
  If so, perchance you seek the fact to hide,
E'en as the proud man shirks, whene'er he dare,
  The poor relation hovering by his side;
But wherefore should you thus disdain to own
  Companionship with honest folks like me?
Since from the humblest cottage to the throne,
  I hold a character for industry.
I love the dwellings of the decent poor,
  For there I shew my face from censure free,
And when I meet you at the cottage door,
  You seldom fail to kindly notice me;
But ah! what sorrows cloud my latter days,
  When my strength fails me and when fades my
      beauty,
Ungrateful man my services repays,
  With calling me vile names when past my duty;
Then after taking from me my good name,
  He casts me out to roam the country round,
Till as a vagrant I am brought to shame,
  Beaten and bruised, and fast in prison bound;
Happy for me there's yet a day to come,
  When tried and purified I shall be free,
And springing forth as from a living tomb,
  The Sage, the Bard, the Wit will honour me;

But I must now resume my pristine name,
　And in a different phase your favour seek.
I've been at court with many a noble dame,
　And unreproved have often kissed her cheek ;
Though mild and plastic in my first address,
　Yet, statesman-like, I'm prone to stick to place ;
To oust me were no easy task " I guess,"
　I dare to tell the Queen so, to her face ;
But though my temperament is soft and bland,
　My warlike ancestors, whene'er they came,
With civil discord filled this happy land.
　And fixed reproach upon their spotted name.
I have some distant relatives, I'm told,
　But they are cross, and never can agree,
So very little intercourse we hold,
　I love not them, nor do they care for me.
My martial ardour perished long ago,
　And now I exercise the healing art ;
No longer will I act as beauty's foe,
　Then never fear to take me to your heart.

ENIGMA III.

I am a little elfish thing,
Born and cradled in the spring,

And these maternal acts are done,
For me in senses more than one;
My infancy is wondrous strange,
And subject to perpetual change;
Black is my robe through every stage,
Till I attain my perfect age;
And then in motley coat I shine,
Lustrous and smooth, and superfine;
But still of such a sober hue,
A Quaker might adopt it too.
My legs, though rather spare and long,
Are agile, unscular and strong,
As I have proved in frequent bound,
When it's my will to clear the ground;
My eyes are wondrous bright and clear,
But ah! my mouth's from ear to ear;
When all the warbling birds combine,
To celebrate Saint Valentine,
I emulate the choral throng,
With my own deep sonorous song.
But those who understood it best,
Assert it comes below my chest;
But howsoever this may be,
It matters not to you or me;
For well I know my welcome voice
Calls on all nature to rejoice;

While every Naiad binds her tresses
With the fresh cooling water-cresses.
I've figured oft in classic story,
And have some claim to martial glory;
My ancestors have been a theme
For a great epic poet's dream!
But boasting now is out of place,
I must confess, to man's disgrace,
We are a persecuted race;
Now some have dared t' assume our name,
Who cannot any kindred claim,
And time has been, when in this nation
They took high military station—
E'en the " Great Captain" of our host
Advanced them to an honoured post;
And though in tactics they'd no part,
He bore them very near his heart.
In battle-field I've heard it said,
They never came, but on parade,
Soft silken forms, in ranks they stood,
Mere carpet knights that ne'er shed blood;
Permit me now in other guise
To pass before your sapient eyes;
Without my aid your favourite steed
Would shamble awkwardly indeed,
And fail you in a case of speed!

Thus if to travel so unable,
'Twere best to leave him in his stable ;
What is my name ? cannot you tell ?
Seek me, like truth, within a well !

ENIGMA IV.

I'm a repulsive being. it is true,
  Yet many bid me welcome to their door ;
And though I am a churl, fair ladies, you
  Full oft consign to me your choicest store.

Lo ! I am changed, and now to me belong
The laugh of revelry. the jovial song ;
Hourly I offer the enchanting cup,
And reckless mortals throng to quaff it up.
Now in another guise you'll plainly see
The first musicians borrow help from me,
And oft in feats equestrian you may trace
High training from a brother of our race.
Behold me now an object of affright,
The wretched culprit trembles at my sight.
Yet for my notice some for years have sighed.
And at my call attend with joy and pride,
Now Proteus-like again I change my form,
The dread of seamen in the ocean storm,

While within view of their desired rest,
I keep them tossing on the billow's breast ;
Till some strong hurricane's opposing power
Shake up my fatal bed, and drive me from the
  shore.

ENIGMA V.

I ROLL upon the gladsome earth
  When Summer fills her lap with flowers ;
I glide upon the icebound flood
  When wintry blasts have stripped the bowers ;
I float upon the waves of air,
  And hold communion with the sky,
And far above the shadowy clouds
  That veil my form from mortal eye ;
I say not 'tis myself to please
  That I these varied rambles take
Unurged, I'm studious of my ease,
  And never an excursion make ;
Oh no! in all my forms I need
  Some stimulant to urge me on ;
Then oft I match the wind in speed,
  Or loiter leisurely along.

ENIGMA VI.

I AM a little tiny elf,
Sportive and harmless by myself;
My course is brief as it is bright,
If nobody obstructs my flight ;
But should I in collision come,
With spirits that provoke their doom,
My form dilates, my victims shrink,
And shrivel at my slightest blink;
No beast more furious than I,
I've made the forest monarch fly.
Fair Ladies, if report speaks true,
My namesakes oft attend on you ;
Beware of their insidious arts,
Yield not too soon your trusting hearts
Lest in the sequel you should pine
At tyranny e'en worse than mine.

ENIGMA VII.

THE guests were merry in Brandon Hall,
   And lamps were blazing bright,
When Emmeline stealthily left the ball,
   At a sign from her own true knight.

Softly she glides through the marble arch,
   With a swift and noiseless tread;
Where the Kingly Oak and the tasseled Larch
   Their shadowy branches spread.

The Moon had hung her cresset high,
   Gilding each arch and tower;
And smiling gazed with placid eye
   On lake and tree and flower.

Fair Emmeline heard the sounds of mirth,
   As the revellers tripped along;
And she thought, "one moonlight walk is worth,
   A life of dance and song."

She hied her to the trysting place,
   But nothing could she spy,
Save the dark, dark pines and the boding owl
   Heavily flapping by.

And thrice upon a name she calls,
   And her cheek was pale with fear;
For she has strayed from her Father's halls,
   And she finds no lover near.

She wanders east, she wanders west,
   She sinks upon her knee;
Distracting terrors fill her breast,
   For she finds herself in *Me*.

But a bugle sounds again! again!
  And her eyes are bright with glee;
She follows straight the signal strain,
  And thus escapes from *Me*.

She springs to meet a stately form,
  That stands by a Linden tree;
But finds herself in her Father's arms,
  As fainting she fails in *Me*.

The recreant Knight had danced all night
  With a lady fair and free;
They are missed from the hall,
And his steed from the stall;
And the wondering guests, as they leave the ball,
  Are instantly plunged in *Me*.

Maidens, my tale this moral bears,
  Beware of treacherie;
Distrust the love that tempts the heart
  To act clandestinelie.

CHARADE I.

My first leads the van of a numerous host,
　　And in argument always has place ;
My next of heraldic distinction can boast,
　　And oft an escutcheon may grace.

Give a head to my third, and lo ! Israel's pride,
　　Her glory, her hope, and her aim ;
My whole may to honour and truth be allied,
　　Or prove but a vain, empty name.

———————

CHARADE II.

My first is of various signification,
And in one is of general use in the nation ;
In a sense more restricted, it hints at the woes
Impending on all academical beaux,
And big wigs forensic heave many a sigh
When they find the unwelcome intruder draws
　　　nigh ;
My next to describe I shall utterly fail,
Unless my grave second will lend me his tail.
And oh ! what a change makes the new situation,
The tail of my first is the head of a nation ;

A nation so populous as to defy
E'en Cocker to number them accurately.
They're a people quite careless of warlike renown,
And shut themselves up in a fortified town;
Yet in seasons of scarcity, I have heard tell,
They will eat through the walls of their own citadel.
And when they're besieged by an enemy's host,
They never do battle, but die at their post,
While their savage invaders so bent upon strife.
That the cry of attack is "war e'en to the knife!"
My puissant total march straight on their way,
And follow their leader in battle array.
Their sappers and miners quite cover the ground,
And spread desolation and rapine around.
Ah, Albion! Albion! land of the free!
May that terrible host never cross thine own sea.

CHARADE III.

Whene'er an argument takes place,
My first's a pleader in the case;
Nor is the privilege more than due.
Since his opponent does so too.
My second is of melting mood,
  And sometimes does a mint of good;

O

But when in contact with the pot,
His temper oft becomes too hot.
Admit my whole within your house,
'Twill do more mischief than a mouse ;
'Twill follow you from room to room,
And even in your wardrobe come.
Oh! never may such dire disgrace
Produce its namesake in your face ;
For it is conscious guilt alone
Can make that countenance your own.

CHARADE IV.

My first, without doubt, is of Roman extraction,
And its welfare depends upon freedom of action ;
With moving on gently, long years it may last,
But oft, like young England, it goes on too fast ;
Then the spendthrift is stopped in its frantic career,
Supplies are withheld, and destruction is near.

My next has a very intelligent face,
Though the footmarks of time in its lines you may
        trace ;
Of many good qualities I am possest,
My notable fingers are seldom at rest.
I'm a truthful narrator, and though I might fail,
In cases of moment, perchance, in my tale,

If you gaze in my round, honest face, you will see
That the fault is another's, and seldom in me.

Though blandly seductive, in seasons of need
My total has oft proved a good friend indeed ;
Yet trust not too much ; with insidious art
It will steal by degrees on your mind and your heart ;
It will fetter your limbs with its adamant chain,
And then, helpless victim, you'll struggle in vain !

CHARADE V.

As my first on four feet always patters about,
You may class it with quadrupeds, there is no doubt:
But as there is scarcely a homestead without it,
Perhaps 'twill suffice to say little about it.

My second is useful in many a line,
But whatever its office, it cannot define.
My third may be ranked as a creature of prey,
With its teeth like a shark's set in double array ;
But though it is said to put hundreds to flight,
It may give you a scratch, but was ne'er known to
    bite.
My whole is a meeting house placed under ground.
Where the guests sit like Quakers, in silence pro-
    found.

CHARADE VI.

To be my first is every statesman's aim ;
To be my first's the end of many a game ;
To be my first's the jockey's pride and boast ;
To be my first and next, might please a host.
My whole is said, without fair truth's infraction,
To be immovable, yet still in action.

CHARADE VII.

RANGE the whole circle of ingenious art,
My comprehensive first still bears a part ;
Nay, stop not there, for much of nature's store
My useful lap exhibits o'er and o'er.

Now change my office, but retain my name,
I lend my aid to many a childish game ;
Nay, full-grown triflers draw me to their side,
And eye the rising heap with joy and pride.

My polished second bears upon its face
A living picture, full of truth and grace ;
The ever-changing figures come and go,
Like shadowy phantoms in the magic show.

The merits of my whole must now be told,
Which, useful in its ornamental fold,
At once adorns, and covers from the cold.

CHARADE VIII.

My first sometimes adorns the form of beauty,
Or hanging pendant at the call of duty,
It aids the pulpit with a decent grace,
Or at the bar presents its solemn face.
Gravely professional, in days of yore,
It walked with famed M. D.'s to sick man's door:
And while he felt the pulse and shook his head,
In sympathy it trembled o'er the bed;
But times are changed, and now my aid I lend,
Not the M.D., but surgeon to befriend.

In other guise it captivates your ears,
Or lifts the raptured spirit to the spheres;
It often designates a brotherhood,
For deeds of evil, or for purpose good.

My next is but an affix to some name,
Whose table-talk is handed down by fame.

My whole in some dark nook its form will fold,
And mostly comes abroad to meet the cold.

CHARADE IX.

My first, prefixed to certain words,
 Oft indicates co-operation.
My next's a connoisseur in birds,
 And of the lesser brute creation.

Without my third, your daintiest meat
 Would really be unfit for table ;
The hungry beggar in the street
Would trample it beneath his feet ;
 To eat it, dogs would be unable.

My fourth, in comprehensive view
 We may a brotherhood proclaim,
Though in it lurks a factious crew,
 Whose discords oft belie the name.

My whole's an intellectual chain,
 More ductile than the finest gold ;
Each precious link enchants the brain
 With visions new, or memories old.

CHARADE X.

My first, of various form and hue,
Cone, circle, square, black, white, red, blue,
 With youth or age is seen.

By night. by day, abroad, at home,
I sit in silence while you roam,
   And wait on clown or queen.

My next holds a distinguished place
Amid the worthies of his race,
   And boasts a glorious name ;
He leads his troops to every clime,
Whose deeds beyond the bounds of time
   Have won a bloodless fame.

Behold my stately third arise,
Crested and crowned to meet the skies,
   The fairest of the fair ;
But soon that lofty head may bow,
And time or vengeance lay it low,
   With brighter things that were !
Reader, you have my whole, no doubt,
And with slight pains will find me out.

CHARADE XII.

At a festival held in this feast-loving nation,
My first always holds a most prominent station.
My next. though attended by sorrow and pain,
Is a point which most people desire to attain.
My whole, if you roam in Australia's bowers.
Will rival. you'll find, the most lovely of flowers.

CHARADE XII.

I SHALL wish you my first, if I find you too near ;
  I shall wish you my next, if I think you too fat.
My third, should you live to the close of next year,
  You will probably meet, so take care of your hat.
My whole is a garment, if rightly I guess,
Much worn in the reign of our merry Queen Bess.

CHARADE XIII.

NOT long with industry abides my first.
  My next's an article in general use.
My dainty third, in fiery regions nursed,
  Gives added zest to Hyson's grateful juice.
My squalid total roams the country round,
For that which industry at home had found.

CHARADE XIV.

WHENEVER you assume my first,
  You give it an exalted station.
My next in fertile India nursed,
  Yields food and wealth to many a nation.
Ladies, my whole's ascribed to you ;
But if you give the men their due,

You'll all acknowledge 'tis but fair
To dub them with an equal share.

CHARADE XV.

To be my first, oh! 'tis a fearful thing!
    But there are some would gladly be my second.
My third, although it pain and trouble bring,
    Yet is a badge of pride and honour reckoned.
My whole is often subject to commotion,
And yet is fast imbedded in the ocean.

CHARADE XVI.

Of various use and form and price,
    My first the housewife knows full well;
Whene'er my second gives advice,
    Take it, or you will ne'er excel.
If in my whole you find good store,
Then, lady, think upon the poor.

CHARADE XVII

My cruel first, with venomed dart
Assailed a lovely woman's heart,

And ah! before the close of day
That breathing form was lifeless clay;
My second seeks to gain attention,
And is of very old invention;
My third is a romantic spot,
Well fitted for a Dryad's grot,
With dripping leaves and mossy seat,
And weeping flowers at your feet.
Curtail my third, and then behold,
My total will a plant unfold.

CHARADE XVIII.

My first, when he maintains his station,
Becomes the head of the creation;
My next oft beautifies the skies,
Yet has no beauty in your eyes.
Oh may my total's fiery dart
Ne'er rankle in your gentle heart!

CHARADE XIX.

My first, though very mean and small,
Has claims to your respect withal.
An Eastern monarch, wise and great,
Beheld it in its low estate,

And raised it to the honoured place
Of Mentor to his numerous race.
You'll find my second in a mine,
Or with his mates upon the line,
Or standing lone in stately pride,
Without one helper by his side.
My third, to do is far from sage,
Especially in feeble age ;
Should e'er such weakness seize your mind,
May you my whole in reason find !

CHARADE XX.

My first with bold, impetuous course,
Comes rushing with resistless force,
    And on, and on, still comes my second.
My whole I do not wish to see
In waiting upon you or me,
    Although a wonder he be reckoned.

CHARADE XXI.

My first leads the van of a numerous host,
    And in argument always takes place ;
My next of heraldic distinction can boast,
    And oft an escutcheon may grace ;

Give a head to my third, and lo! Israel's pride,
   Her glory, her hope, and her aim!
My whole may to honour and truth be allied,
   Or prove but a vain, empty name.

CHARADE XXII.

SMALL, but potential is my first,
   A very self-sufficient elf;
But when it is by wisdom nurst,
   It leads to honour, fame, or pelf.
My second, dead to present times,
   Always refers to actions past.
If you're my whole, you'll say these rhymes
   Have o'er me but a thin veil cast.

CHARADE XXIII.

My first was the chief actor in a royal tragedy :
My next and third a pendant that no one likes to
   see ;
My fourth, I trust, a happy pair in legal union
   bound,
And oft in their vocation there, may on the line be
   found.

My whole, though surely not a fish, yet scaly I
    define,
And often figures in a dish at table when you dine.

CHARADE XXIV.

My first's a superstitious rite,
    Nursed in the lap of Rome ;
My second, if you look aright,
    Surrounds the rural home ;
My total is a barbarous deed,
O'er which all gentle hearts must bleed.

CHARADE XXV.

Clothed in my first my whole behold,
    A wretched outcast old and poor.
Ah, once how jaunty, gay and bold,
    He swaggered at the tavern door ;
Would he attend to wisdom's voice,
    And from my next a lesson take,
How would he make those hearts rejoice,
    Which now with shame and sorrow ache.

CHARADE XXVI.

My first has a strong inclination to flirt,
   Though the day of its triumphs is over;
A shrewd Irish beggar, as some folks assert,
   Was my second, and " living in clover;"
Should you sigh for repose, my third you should do,
   Where nothing exists to excite you ;
But if to my whole you are wishing to go,
   Persuade some old don to invite you.

REBUS I.

Awaked by my whole in the dead of the night,
No doubt you would be in a terrible fright;
But take off my head, and then, if you please,
You may revel in visions of butter and cheese.
Behead me once more, and then, if you're wary,
I may serve you for years, and be yet stationary.

REBUS II.

Complete, my glory is in revolution;
Behead me, I may give you a contusion ;
Behead again, and if your cook has skill,
She'll make a turncoat of me 'gainst my will.

REBUS III.

I am the only thing a brave man fears;
Strike off my head, a Scottish home appears ;
Again behead me, I shall then declare
What monsieur often calls his favourite fair.

REBUS IV.

Should you meet with my whole when you're
        taking the air,
Behead me and mount me as soon as you dare ;
Behead me once more, if you've surgical skill,
For while I'm alive I must always be ill.

REBUS V.

I am the navigator's trusty guide,
And oft the tourist woos me to his side ;
Strike off my head, and if I stand at bay,
Take to your heels, 'twill be the safest way ;
Behead once more, and in my name you'll find
That which debases or exalts the mind.

REBUS VI.

Dear ladies, I own 'tis my trade to deceive,
But cut off my head and I beg you'll believe
  I shall then prove a very warm friend ;
    Behead me once more,
    Should you live to fourscore,
  To my hint you will gladly attend.

THE END.

www.ingramcontent.com/pod-product-compliance
Lightning Source LLC
Chambersburg PA
CBHW030821270326
41928CB00007B/844